NOBLESSE

Noblesse Oblige

AN ENQUIRY INTO THE IDENTIFIABLE CHARACTERISTICS OF THE ENGLISH ARISTOCRACY

by

ALAN S. C. ROSS

NANCY MITFORD

EVELYN WAUGH

'STRIX'

CHRISTOPHER SYKES

and

JOHN BETJEMAN

With an Introduction by Ned Sherrin

Illustrated by

OSBERT LANCASTER

OXFORD
UNIVERSITY PRESS

Great Clarendon Street, Oxford OX2 6DP

Oxford University Press is a department of the University of Oxford.
It furthers the University's objective of excellence in research, scholarship,
and education by publishing worldwide in

Oxford New York

Auckland Bangkok Buenos Aires Cape Town Chennai
Dar es Salaam Delhi Hong Kong Istanbul Karachi Kolkata
Kuala Lumpur Madrid Melbourne Mexico City Mumbai Nairobi
São Paulo Shanghai Singapore Taipei Tokyo Toronto

and an associated company in Berlin

Oxford is a registered trade mark of Oxford University Press
in the UK and in certain other countries

First published by Hamish Hamilton 1956
Published in Penguin Books 1959
First issued as an Oxford University Press paperback 1989
Reissued as an Oxford Language Classic 2002

Introduction by Ned Sherrin © Oxford University Press 2002

British Library Cataloguing in Publication Data

Data available

Library of Congress Cataloging in Publication Data

Data available

ISBN 0-19-860520-X

1 3 5 7 9 10 8 6 4 2

Printed in Great Britain by
Clays Ltd, St Ives plc

NOTE

THE contributions to *Noblesse Oblige* by Professor Alan Ross, Miss Nancy Mitford, and Mr. Evelyn Waugh appeared in *Encounter*. Professor Ross's article is a condensed and simplified version of his 'Linguistic class-indicators in present-day English' which appeared in 1954 in the Finnish philological periodical *Neuphilologische mitteilungen*. A shorter version of 'Strix's' contribution appeared in *The Spectator*. Mr. John Betjeman's *How to Get On in Society* is taken from *A Few Late Chrysanthemums* and is reprinted by kind permission of the author and Messrs. John Murray.

1066

1500

Diagram showing the gradual infiltration by non-U elements of a U peerage passing in the female line.

1600

1730.

1900

1956

CONTENTS

INTRODUCTION

This 'Enquiry into the identifiable characteristics of the English Aristocracy' was one of Nancy Mitford's most spectacular 'teases'—or, as she wrote to Violet Hammersley on the 15th March 1955, 'it will contain a whole volley of teases.' Two years before she had written to Evelyn Waugh:

> I had a nice chat with a Professor Ross. He is off to North Norway where he expects to find some Danish dialect hitherto lost. He wanted to see me about note paper and so on. He has written a paper about all that for some Finnish university. I told him he should publish it in London, under the title of *Are you a Hon?* He would make his fortune. He blanched.

The earnest Ross was a Philologist, Professor of Linguistics at the University of Birmingham. The results of his research into Upper Class English Usage were to be published in a learned Finnish Journal, the Bulletin of the Neo-Philological Society of Helsinki (*Neuphilologische Mitteilungen*).

It is not clear why Professor Ross offered his research to the Finns. Maybe they asked him? Perhaps he stopped off there on his way back from North Norway? But in his paper he argues that:

> Nearly all English people are snobs of one or two kinds—true snobs or inverted snobs. In this respect England differs from Finland and Iceland and resembles Spain or pre-war Hungary.

Ross draws on a short article by the late Professor H. C. Wyld explaining: 'He was well equipped for the task, for he was both a gentleman and a philologist.' However, he admits that Wyld's conclusions were 'perhaps a little old-fashioned for instance, the dictum 'no gentleman goes on a bus . . . is one which most gentlemen have to neglect'.

(Not Lord Curzon who stepped on a bus just once and complained when the driver declined to take him to Carlton House Terrace. However, two of Curzon's prejudices might have found favour with Ross. 'Gentlemen do not take soup at luncheon' and 'Gentlemen never wear brown in London'; but not perhaps his observation 'Dear me, I never knew the lower classes had such white skins.')

Another of Ross's sources is R. W. Chapman's 'excellent' *Names, designations and appellations*, published in 1946. Ross points out that: 'Chapman does not specifically deal with Non-U usages,' but he assumes that since, 'his enumeration is considered as exhaustive . . . usages divergent from those given are Non-U.'

Delving further into history Ross cites J. Walker's *Critical Pronouncing Dictionary and expositor of the English Language* (1791) 'in which he is clearly trying to differentiate between U and Non-U usage'. Sadly for Ross, 'nearly all the points mentioned by him only one hundred and thirty years ago—are now "dead" and without class significance.'

Nearly 50 years on the same might be said of many of the judgements passed down in *Noblesse Oblige*, though there is no doubt that an underlying snobbery survives with different yardsticks.

In recent years John Major has been scornfully 'placed' as a man who wears his shirt tucked inside his pants; and Alan Clark has quoted Michael Joplin, dismissing Michael Heseltine as 'a man who bought his own furniture'.

The 'tease' was Nancy Mitford's delight and often her most

subversive weapon. As an oldest child whose unique position in the family was sabotaged when her sister Pamela was born she converted everything said, painful or simply irritating into a joke, 'How we shrieked!' When other siblings arrived they were too young to be proper companions. She converted her isolation from them into comedy. Her bright wit and sharp tongue made her a natural attacker.

Pamela Mitford, her first victim lacked the challenging imagination of her sisters—though in much later life she did bring off one spectacular 'tease'. Moving her household from Switzerland to Gloucestershire she applied to bring her rare Alpenzeller hens into the country. The ministry refused to issue a permit, 'So', she said 'I simply brought in a dozen eggs and hatched them.'

Back in the nursery she was weakened by an attack of polio. Nancy, whose teasing campaign began when she thought she had lost the affection of her Nanny to the new baby, set out to make her life miserable in spite of grown-up reprimands: 'You've *got* to be kind to Pam, she's ill.' A pattern was established. The next sister, Diana, was terrified as a child of leaving home. Nancy would say, 'I've been talking about you to Muv and Farve. We were saying how good it would be for you to go away to school.' The three younger girls, Unity, Jessica, and Deborah were easy victims. 'Do you realise, you three, how awful the middle syllables of your names are—Nit, Sic and Bor?'

As Nancy grew older she risked teasing her explosive father, a more dangerously volatile victim, and her mother. Her portrait of Lady Redesdale in *The Blessing* provoked an injured protest and the reply, 'Oh, Goodness, I thought it would make you laugh. Of course,' she wrote, 'the trouble is that I see my childhood (in fact most of my life) as a hilarious joke.'

Evelyn Waugh called her 'an agitator of genius' and Harold Acton wrote 'she could not resist a childish temptation to

shock, more mischievous than malicious'. She upset America by
saying that John Wilkes Booth was her favourite character
because he had killed Lincoln, 'the most odious character in history. When I read *The Day Lincoln was Shot* I was dreadfully
afraid he (Booth) might go to the wrong theatre.' She infuriat-
ed her adored France with an article which justified the execu-
tions of Marie-Antoinette as a traitress. Her reward was to be
cut dead by Prince Pierre of Monaco.

To stumble on Professor Ross while she was between two of
her historical books *Madame de Pompadour* (1954) and *Voltaire
in Love* three years later offered a diversionary treasure trove of
teases. She could scatter a rich deposit of snobbery on the
socially insecure and ambitious and enjoy the joke in the company of friends sensitive to the nuances of class, behaviour, and
pronunciation like Evelyn Waugh, John Betjeman, and Osbert
Lancaster.

The joke was bound to spread quickly. It provided instant
ammunition for glossy magazines and popular newspapers
which enjoy playing games of lists. Who is in or out? What
is Up or Down? What is correct or incorrect? Gauche or
sophisticated? Modern or dated? Fashionable or unfashion-
able?

When she met Ross at luncheon with an American friend she
made a polite enquiry about his work. Her latest biographer,
Mary Lovell, suggests that 'her exaggerated [Mitford] drawl
was what Eliza's cockney was to Higgins; a prime subject to
study'. Ross had already decided on his title 'U and Non-U
denoting upper-class and non-upper-class-usage.' Reassured
that his paper was in English she begged him to send her a
copy. When the proof arrived she was delighted to see her
novel *The Pursuit of Love* quoted in a footnote as an authority
for English upper-class speech (1945 edn. p. 31).

It does not survive in *Noblesse Oblige* as edited by Nancy,
except as a page reference. It is the famous passage in which

Uncle Matthew attacks the vulgarizing effects of education on Fanny's vocabulary.

> Education! I was always led to suppose that no educated person ever spoke of notepaper, and yet I hear Fanny asking Sadie for notepaper. What is this education? Fanny talks about mirrors and mantelpieces, handbags and perfume, she takes sugar in her coffee, has a tassel on her umbrella, and I have no doubt that, if she is fortunate enough to catch a husband, she will call his father and mother Father and Mother. Will the wonderful education she is getting make up to the unhappy brute for all these endless pinpricks? Fancy hearing one's wife talk about notepaper - the irritation!

Nancy was enraptured by Ross's serious academic approach to a topic which she had treated with laughter.

Then Stephen Spender, co-editor of *Encounter* commissioned her to write her own article. On 15 March 1955 she wrote to Violet Hammersley— another regular victim of her teases:

> I have been asked to write a hugely long article for *Encounter* on the English aristocracy. Can't quite decide, but if I do it it will contain volleys of teases. It's a series—French, German, Italian and Spanish too by various experts. I rather wish I'd been allotted the French, really only it might have killed Mme. Costa (Countess Costa de Beauregard) . . . Do help with the aristos. I need lots of ideas. Thought I'd say the vast majority belong to C of E, the few who believe in God are R.C.'s science and Ox Group. Also stress the fact that they would rather do anything—even wash-up and cook—sooner than work for a living. If money doesn't fall from heaven they cheerfully . . . do without? One thing I'm asked is who are the eccentrics of this age? Who? . . . HELP.

The day before she had written to Mark Ogilvie Grant, 'My article is brilliant . . . I lovingly linger over it, adding telling phrases.'

Nearly a year earlier she had spotted the potential for re-publication in hard cover. She wrote to the bookseller Heywood Hill:

> My crazy friend Prof. Ross has written such a lovely pamphlet for *la société neo-philologique de Helsinki* printed in Finland but written in English, on upper class usage in England. Entitled 'Linguistic class-indicators in present day English'. It has sentences like 'The ideal U-address (U stands for upper class) is P.A.R, where P is a place name. A is a describer (manor, court, house etc.) and R the name of a county . . . but today few gentlemen can maintain this standard and they often live in houses with non-U names such as Fairfields or El Nido.' (What will the Finns make of it?)
>
> Anyway it seems to me a natural for the Xmas market, illustrated by O. Lancaster and entitled Are You U? I've suggested this to the Prof. (who may think it dreadfully infra dig) and I've told him if the idea appeals to him to send you a copy and you would perhaps advise about a publisher.
>
> It is dreadfully funny throughout because written in serious scientific style. I'm glad to say P of L is one of the source books. He is a great new character in my life and a card if ever there was one—U himself and in my expert opinion he has got everything right but ONE.

(In her essay she hints that this might be Ross's question. 'Can a non-U speaker become a U-speaker?' to which he answers 'no').

By May she had heard of Ross's misgivings and wrote to Hill; 'Prof. Ross most indignant at the idea that his Finnish pamphlet on U speakers might be turned into an Xmas best seller. Oh, what a pity.'

However, on Spender's encouragement she put pen to paper for *Encounter*. She wrote to Heywood Hill:

> I lovingly cook away at it all day and I think it is the best thing I have ever done. It's a sort of anthology of teases—

something for everybody. I think it will be safer to be in Greece when it appears.

The reader will judge the validity of the Ross/Mitford contention that it is possible to identify true members of the aristocracy by behaviour, words, and expressions—the use of fish knives, milk poured before tea, 'notepaper', 'mirror', 'settee', and 'serviette'. Propelled by the enthusiasm with which Nancy Mitford bounces her jokes along the idea is appealing. Where Professor Ross is earnest and methodical Mitford is exuberant and infectious and when later she invited a riposte from Evelyn Waugh the marriage of two wits is as intoxicating as an exchange between Beatrice and Benedick.

The joke was, however, one in which Nancy Mitford did to some extent believe, if not as seriously as Waugh. Selena Hastings has pointed out in her biography:

> She was not a snob in the sense of looking up to someone solely because he had money or Rank: but Nancy was never a member of the public. She saw herself as special and apart; her friends were special and apart; she believed in privilege and tradition, in old-established families in big houses surrounded by acres of land . . . she once told Heywood (Hill) her idea of Utopia 'consists of cottagers, happy in their cottages while I am being happy in the Big House.' In short she believed that everyone should know his place, and in language was to be found one of the crucial lines of demarcation.

The publication of the article in *Encounter* in 1955 did indeed cause a sensation—any accessible barometer of class is likely to promise storms over England. The debate was furious. Raw nerves were touched. In a letter to her mother she wrote 'I went to WHS here yesterday—manager dashed at me saying all sold out the first day. Heywood usually sells 20 had sold over 100 last week.'

Her correspondence was hectic. She told Alvilde Lees-Milne:

Everybody now is furious—Frogs, Greeks and English—
and Geoffrey (Gilmour) says the only place left for me is
America where they can't read. One man wrote (to
Encounter), 'I often go to the Guards' Club and there they
generally say cheers to something before drinking. Since the
article they still say it but with some reference to Miss M.'
Can't you hear them? To hell with Miss M. Another wrote
to me, 'my secretary has just read your article and refuses to
type a letter to you.' I wrote back is your secretary a
Duchess?

She wrote to her mother that she had had hundreds of letters:

Mostly fans, though some abuse—a friend in London sent
me a telegram saying lunch Saturday and the girl on the telephone said, 'as this is Miss Nancy Mitford should we not put
LUNCHEON?'

Meanwhile she had sent her *Encounter* essay to Waugh.

'Dearest Nancy,   1 Sept 1955

Thank you very much for sending me *Encounter*. I read
your essay with keen relish. I wish it had been much longer.

The exposition of Fortinbrass (the imaginary peer she
invents to illustrate her argument) is first class: also your
rebuke to the upper class for their capitulations . . .

Nancy confessed to Christopher Sykes that she liked Waugh's
next point 'that each family invents its own U-Talk and thinks
all other common.' 'I wish I'd thought of it myself.' As Waugh
put it:

I wish your Upper Class usage had touched on a point that
has long intrigued me. Almost everyone I know has some
personal antipathy which they condemn as middle-class

quite irrationally. My mother-in-law believes it is middle class to decant claret. Lord Beauchamp thought it m.c. *not* to decant champagne (into jugs). Your 'notepaper' is another example. I always say 'luncheon' but you will find 'lunch' used in every generation for the last 80 years (by) unimpeachable sources. There are very illiterate people like Percy Brownlow who regard all correct grammar as a middle class affectation. Ronnie Knox blanches if one says, 'docile' with a long 'o'. I correct my children if they say 'bike' for bicycle. I think everyone has certain fixed ideas that have no relation to observed usage. The curious thing is that, as you say, an upper class voice is always unmistakable though it may have every deviation of accent and vocabulary. Compare for instance the late Lord Westmoreland, Salisbury, Curzon. A phonetician would find no point of resemblance in their speech.

Herbaceous borders came in as an economy. The first drawing in of horns when potting and bedding out became too expensive . . .

The plan for Waugh's reply (*An Open Letter to the Hon Mrs Peter Rodd (Nancy Mitford) on a Very Serious Subject*) was quickly afoot. It soon ran into trouble when publishers attempted to deal with Waugh.

15 October 1955 Pier's Court.
Dearest Nancy,

Thank you for sending me Hamilton's letter. I can't deal with a man who, not knowing me at all, refers to me by my Christian name, but I will send *you* a proof of my letter when I get one. At present only a manuscript exists which I have sent to *Encounter*. It is about 4,000 words long. Except that I expose you as a hallucinated communist agent there is nothing in it to hurt. I deal with heraldry, genealogy, precedence, conception of 'gentleman', the finances of aristocracy

and such important topics. Very little about verbal usage.
That was a minor issue in your article and I think it very
morbid of your readers to attach such importance to it.

Morbid, he may have thought it—but it was the undeniable
selling and talking point for *Encounter* and *Noblesse Oblige*. He
continued:

Professor Ross did not seem to me to do much except borrow from Uncle Matthew and the old Society for Pure
English Tracts and to invent the expression 'non-U' which I
regard as vulgar in the extreme—like V.D. for venereal dis-
ease and P.C. for postcard. 'U Book' would be a dreadful title.

This is writing paper or letter paper. Single sheets are
notepaper. Pray note 'Glos' on the engraving (and always
write the departments of France in future). No 'S et O'.

Nancy replied sharply:

For Seine et Oise, I never in my LIFE put S and O or A and
M on letters—what an awful idea. As bad as U-quite.

Waugh confided grumpily to his diary:

I wrote a long refutation of Nancy's mischievous article in
Encounter dealing very little with her glossary of plebian
expressions which has caused all the stir, and much with her
misrepresentations of the English class system. Mr H.
Hamilton (who impudently refers to me as 'Evelyn' in his
correspondence) wants to issue a booklet on the subject.

Correspondence continued to pour in. In September Nancy
wrote to Raymond Mortimer 'A letter from Willie (Maugham)
saying he can't be U as he says toilet paper. Ugh.' Six days later
she told her mother Lady Redesdale:

A flood of letters re *Encounter*—mostly fans, though some
abuse. 'I am circulating it in the monastery—the Prior much

impressed by it . . .' It was wicked old Spender, eye on sales, who egged me on to do the U stuff . . . I'm pleased as they gave me 3 times their usual, so I feel I've earned it.

The rumblings about publication of the book continued—with a deal of social jousting. On 20 October Waugh wrote to his agent A.D. Peters:

> Dear Pete, the 'Aristocracy' article has gone to *Encounter*. I think as a matter of prestige that if it is used in an anthology of snobbery by H. Hamilton it should somehow be made plain that it was a book by Nancy and me with a few press cuttings thrown in. Please don't quote the foregoing sentence to Hamilton or it will be repeated to my discredit. Can you convey the sense of it, as coming from you? In fact Nancy's article and mine together, alone, would make an excellent pamphlet. I answer her at every point. Prof. Ross is a bore . . .

The next day he wrote to Nancy in an even more tetchy vein.

> Darling Nancy, The Editor of the *Encounter* has mistakenly sent me a letter written to Mr Weidenfeld. He says: 'I have looked through our correspondence and I find that we have not promised the aristocracy series to anyone else. So you can have first call—though, as I say, it is going to be many months before the series is anything like complete, when we have other articles in, we can write to authors and tell them our plans.'
>
> It is a strange underworld you have led me into.
>
> I have instructed Peters to make it plain that *Encounter* have only first serial rights and are not empowered to make any arrangements about book publication. Perhaps you will do the same and also warn your friend Hamilton of these subversive Jewish plots. Or is Hamilton also a Jew? I have heard it suggested.

In another letter, dated the same day Waugh announces a discovery:

Look. I have found some old note-paper [*sic*] with Glos. in full.
   You will have found my letter exposing the Kristol–Weidenfeld plot. [Irving Kristol was the founder and co-editor with Spender of *Encounter*.] I thought it great impudence of Kristol to think he can arrange our publishing for us . . . your letter of reply is not very honest about your red sympathies, is it? . . . If there is anything in my article you think impolite, say and of course I will change it. I think you miss the point about putative parentage. I merely meant pedigrees were not infallible in attributing character, e.g. noses. There are only about four shapes of nose. People say, 'look at the Fortinbras nose.' Rot, really. . . .

Waugh's suggestion that Nancy might like him to withdraw anything impolite amused her.

How I've been shrieking! The PLOT . . . I've withdrawn the reply but you must also change your piece. You know I am not a Communist, Evelyn, don't you? . . . Think of me as a Christian—*early* if you like.

On 2 November he capitulated:

I have cut out all reference to communism and attributed your class-war battle cry to your admiration for Lloyd George . . .

Nancy replied:

Yes, that's perfect. I know you can't tell the difference between Lloyd George and Stalin, but other people can.

Waugh continued:

I haven't changed the 'Hon' bit because after all it was you who made the Hon joke public property, even if you didn't originate it. It will always be linked with your name, not with the Duchess or the Communist.

Members of Nancy's family reacted in various ways. Her youngest sister, Debo, the Duchess of Devonshire, wrote to *Encounter* to correct him on the subject of 'Hons'—a word used in *The Pursuit of Love* to describe a secret society of the youngest Mitford/Radlett children. Waugh had pointed out in his essay that Nancy was 'Queen of the Hons' and reminds her:

> You were at the vital age of twelve when your father suc-
> ceeded to his peerage and until less than a year before that
> there was little likelihood of his ever succeeding. It was a
> great day for 'Hons' when you and your merry sisters
> acquired that prefix of nobility. Hitherto it had been the most
> shadowy of titles, never spoken and rarely written. You
> brought it to light, emphasised and aspirated, and made a
> glory of it . . . Anyway at that impressionable age an indeli-
> ble impression was made; Hons were unique and lords were
> rich.

The Duchess was quick to point out that Waugh was in error. In their secret childhood language ('Honnish' or 'Boudledidge') 'Hon' was derived from 'Hen'. Debo and Jessica the two youngest Mitford girls were keen on chickens. They earned pocket money looking after their mother's. They originally called their secret club the Society of Hens. Indeed they often called each other 'Hen' until Decca's death in 1996. 'Hen' later became 'Hon'. Breaking the club's rules made one a Counter Hon. The H. was always pronounced in Hon as it is in Hen. It was never, as Waugh assumed a society for girls entitled to the prefix Honourable.

Writing in 2002 the Duchess remembers, 'The Hons were a club, my sister Decca, myself, the daughter of the gardener and sometimes some Honorary Hons.'

It wasn't only Waugh who had misread the reference. In

Noblesse Oblige

January 1956 Nancy wrote to the Duchess of Devonshire:

> Dear 9 [she always pretended that her youngest sister had a
> mental age of 9—another tease]. I've just had a letter from
> my Dutch translator saying will the 'the cave of the nobles'
> do for *Huns* cupboard? I think you'd better write and explain
> that it is a hen house—that'll fox him.

In 1957 when both Waugh and Nancy Mitford had grown tired
of the joke it erupts again in a letter from Waugh, prompted by
the Duchess.

> Darling Nancy, I saw Debo last week. I feel it my duty to tell
> you that she is spreading a very damaging story about you:
> that you have allowed yourself to be photographed by the
> television. Of course I do not believe it nor does anyone who
> knows and loves you, but I think you should scotch this slan-
> der before it spreads to people who might do so. It would
> entirely destroy your reputation as 'U-governess'.

Nancy's husband, Peter Rodd—they were to be divorced in
1957—wrote ungallantly to the *Daily Telegraph*:

> Sir, There has been a good deal of discussion by your sillier
> contemporaries about words which are 'sub-U and Non-U'. I
> am sorry to see that this sad little controversy has seeped
> into your columns. It is very vulgar . . . I can only beseech
> you to refrain from further exposure of decaying tripe. Yours
> faithfully, Peter Rodd.

Diana Mosley bewailed, 'the horror and vulgarity of the whole
notion'.

From San Francisco the Communist Mitford, Jessica, wrote
to her mother that the *New York Times* had reported that
10,000 copies of *Noblesse Oblige* had been sold there in a single
week. 'What's that about?' she asked.

Noblesse Oblige launched Jessica Mitford on her writing

career. When her mother explained, she picked up not on the Aristocracy but on the idea that language was what marked the upper class from the others.

An idea flashed into my mind; was this not also true of the Communist Left? Why not a booklet on Left usage, patterned after Nancy's book? The annual P.W. drive was underway. [P.W. *People's World* was the West Coast equivalent of the *Daily Worker* which party members supported by fund-raising.] If I wrote my booklet, charged 50 cents a copy and managed to sell 100 of them, I would make my quota for the year.

With a bow to Stephen Potter she called her pamphlet *Lifemanship* or *How to Become a Precisely-Because Man; an Investigation into current L (or Left Wing) usage.* Somewhat to her surprise the comrades showed a sense of humour: 'On a couple of occasions in the past I had been brought up on charges of making jokes in Party meetings.'

After conscious testing of the water, 'The response was nothing short of thrilling.' In England Philip Toynbee published some examples of 'L-speech' in the *Observer*.

Decca's 'tease' contrasted reasonable forms of speech with left wing clichés:

e.g. 'An L-man does not speak up at a meeting he contributes to a discussion.'
'Suggesting a bum plan' = 'Projecting an incorrect perspective'. There was also a section requiring answers to a series of questions.
e.g. 'What is Wall Street drunk with?'
'Temporary but illusory success' (correct)
'Old Grandad' (incorrect)
'What must we establish with the toiling masses and their allies?'
(a)   Closer ties

   (b)   Firmer links
   (c)   Durable alliances
   (d)   Unshakeable idealogical ties/links/alliances.

Stapled at home by Decca's children and often delivered by them, Decca was triumphant. Orders poured in from Bookshops, libraries and individuals all over the United States, from Canada, England and Australia. A Japanese student wrote from Tokyo, 'I find it is much interesting and feel the Left people has same usage both sides Pacific Ocean.' The *People's World* concluded: 'The idea that the American Left can laugh at itself appears to be an encouraging one.' And a surprise, I shouldn't wonder.

The contributions of Peter Fleming (strix in the *Spectator*) on *Posh Lingo* and Christopher Sykes *What U-Future* do not match the style and high spirits of Mitford and Waugh. Strix deals mainly with the Army. Sykes forecasts usage in 2055. 'U' becomes 'T' for Top People. A laboured piece.

It is un-T to bring your dinner wrapped in newspaper or a coloured cloth. T-people always bring it in a briefcase but would consider a picnic basket as vulgarly ostentatious.

On the other hand Osbert Lancaster's illustrations retain their freshness and pertinence; and John Betjeman's *How to get on in Society* is an evergreen distillation of all that Professor Ross was looking for. I am indebted to Bevis Hillier for background information on Betjeman's poem, its genesis, and some consequences which he sets out in the second volume of his Betjeman biography.

When Betjeman was (as he pronounced it) 'Literary advazer' to Lady Rhonda's 'Taime and Taide' the most enjoyable part of his job was setting some of the weekly literary competitions. On 29th December 1951 he asked readers to add a final verse to his poem *How to get on in Society*. It was already in existence in 1949 when Randolph Churchill, who had heard the first line ('Phone for the fish knives, Norman') from someone, asked him for a copy—so the fascination for words and phrases that upper class people were not supposed to use was already abroad six years before Ross's paper.

In his report on the *Time and Tide* competition, on 19 January 1952 Betjeman wrote that he had been 'dazzled by yards of splendid verses from over a hundred entrants'. I have followed Bevis Hillier's selection. One competitor 'Μορεν sent in not one final verse but an entire poem. Betjeman said he thought it was better than his own. Hillier quotes the first two stanzas:

Would you care for a smoke or a sherry?
The cocktail cabinet's there.
No, the savoury spread and the vitamin bread's
In a cubby hole under the stair.

Has uncle gone out on his cycle?
He left making terrible sounds,
Saying 'Just what the medico ordered'
I'm afraid he'll get lost in the grounds.

Betjeman gave the first prize to 'H.M.B.':

Your pochette's on the pouffe by the cake-stand
Beneath your fur-fabric coatee.
Now, before we remove to the study
Let me pass you these chocs from Paris.

H.M.B.'s alternative offer was just as neat and concentrated:

Should you need a shampoo or a hair-do
You have only to push on the bell;
My personal maid comes from Monte
And does a Marcel very well.

I share Bevis Hillier's enthusiasm for one of the five runners up—J.A. Gere:

Just one wee portion of gâteau?
I made it with my own fair hand.
And—though I says it as shouldn't—
My menfolk have voted it grand.

but perhaps 'though I says it as shouldn't' is just too obviously 'below stairs' to qualify. C.S.W.'s honourable mention was well earned,

Late dinner—D.J.—at half-seven
(There are gaspers and lights in the box)
Meanwhile, squattez-vous with the mags, dear,
And a glass of port-wine and some chocs.

Across the Atlantic in *The New Yorker* the American humorous poet Ogden Nash joined in the game in September 1956 with his poem 'M.S. Found Under A Serviette in a Lovely Home'. 'Our outlook is totally different from that of our American cousins, who have never had an aristocracy. Americans relate all effort, all work and all of life itself to the dollar. Their talk is of nothing but dollars. The English seldom sit happily chattering for hours on end about pounds.' (Nancy Mitford in *Noblesse Oblige*.)

Dear Cousin Nancy:
You probably never heard of me or Cousin Beauregard or Cousin Yancey,
But since you're claiming kin all the way across the ocean, we figure you must be at least partwise Southern,
So we consider you not only our kith and kin but also our kithin' couthern.
I want to tell you, when Cousin Emmy Lou showed us your piece it stopped the conversation flat,
Because I had twenty dollars I wanted to talk about, and Cousin Beauregard had ten dollars he wanted to talk about, and Cousin Yancey didn't have any dollars at all, and he wanted to talk about that.
But Cousin Emmy Lou looked over her spectacles, which the common people call glasses,

And she offered us a dollar to stop talking about dollars and
start talking about the English upper classes.
Cousin Beauregard wanted to know why the English aris-
tocracy was called English when most of their names were
French to begin with,
And now anybody with an English name like Hobbs or
Stobbs has to accumulate several million of those pounds
they seldom chat about, to buy his way in with.
Cousin Yancey said he could understand that—the St.
Aubyns beat the hell out of the Hobbses in 1066—but
there was a more important point that he could not deter-
mine,
Which is why the really aristocratic English aristocrats have
names that are translated from the German.
Cousin Emmy Lou is pretty aristocratic herself; in spite of
her weakness for hog jowl and potlikker, she is noted for
her highborn pale and wan flesh,
And where most people get gooseflesh she gets swan flesh,
And she said she thought you ought to know that she had
been over the royal roster
And she had spotted at least one imposter.
She noticed that the wicked Queen said, 'Mirror, mirror on
the wall' instead of 'Looking glass, looking glass on the
wall,' which is perfectly true,
So the wicked Queen exposed herself as not only wicked but
definitely non-U.
After that, we all loosened our collars
And resumed our conversation about dollars.

Nancy wrote to him immediately: 'I love you, Mr Ogden Nash'.

The most reasoned riposte was Paul Dehn's in *Punch* (trig-
gered by *Encounter*) which he called *A Woman of a Certain
Class:*

I have only kept silent so long because the English gentleman in me shies, like one of my own hunters, at the idea of betraying a woman—my *noblesse* refuges to *oblige*.

He goes on to quote etymological corrections for the precedence of 'home' over 'house', 'greens' over 'vegetables', 'sweet' over 'pudding', 'toilet' over 'lavatory'; defends 'serviette' and explains the significance of 'luncheon' and 'dinner'. He has a good deal of fun at the expense of the 'Indo-European' Mitfords 'arrived from God knows where behind the Karakorams' compared to 'the Old English Dehns.' It produced an explosion from Waugh in a letter to Nancy Mitford on 29 December:

> I don't suppose you see *Punch*. I enclose an example of the banal products of your communist tract. We have scotched the jewish plot, but we must watch out for 'Hamish Hamilton' who may wish to adulterate our contribution with trash of this kind.

He refers again to the controversy about Scotch, Scottish or Scots and finishes:

> But have a care you do not step outside the limits of polite conversation into those of the King's English. That is the study of a lifetime and it is too late for you to start. The charm of your writing depends on your refusal to recognise a distinction between girlish chatter and literary language. You will be lost if you fall into pedantry. Stick to pillow cases v. pillow slips.

Noblesse Oblige was published early in 1956 and by now U-fatigue was beginning to set in. Professor Ross resented Nancy's making fun of his academic thesis and when Nancy herself wrote to Hugh Thomas in February, she seems to need to justify its seven day wonder.

> Yes, can you beat the U-fuss? People now round on me, saying what a bore it all is, but really they've only got to leave off. However, if it stops the corruption of our language by

Americanisms it will have done some good, perhaps only snobbishness can stop it. We have no *Académie* and my Grandmother used to say, 'Mothers are the guardians of the English language.' (The fathers were supposed to be too much inclined to bring home military or parliamentary slang and clichés.)

She wrote to Evelyn Waugh in June in a lighter vein:

Can you get over them going *on* with U? I mean we've really had enough—even I have and you know how one loves one's own jokes. As we are on the subject the best was, 'I'm dancing with tears in my eyes 'cos the girl in my arms isn't U.'

Harold Acton judged that in the end the article diminished Nancy.

The squib fired off by Nancy in playful mood continued to send hissing sparks, long after Nancy became bored with it. Unfortunately the pother it caused helped to falsify the popular image of her character.

Some of her U-shibboleths she came to take seriously nevertheless, not only in post-prandial argument and I suspect that her stubborn prejudice against her early novels might partly be due to the inclusion of non-U words.

In *Highland Fling* she had written, 'Every mirror was besieged by women powdering their noses'; 'over the mantelpiece hung a Victorian mirror'; 'an enormous Gothic masterpiece of pitch-pine'. In *Christmas Pudding*: 'Like most people who write for a living he hated writing letters, and moreover seldom had any notepaper in his lodgings.' She complained to Waugh that she had practically to re-write *Pigeon Pie* which was about to be re-published '[It is] full of mirrors, mantelpieces and handbags, etc. Don't tell my public or I'm done for.'

'U' and 'non-U' is best regarded as a joke, a 'Mitford tease' which touched the public imagination (or lack of it) to an unusual degree. The markers laid down are imprecise and change from generation to generation making them an unreliable yardstick but a convenient diversion.

To Waugh's irritation his dissertations on the aristocracy did not excite the public as did the exploitable tabloid trick of U and non-U. The subjects of class will always hold a fascination for the British. One enduring piece of successful, subsequent revue writing confirms it—John Law's evergreen sketch performed by John Cleese, Ronnie Barker and Ronnie Corbett on *The Frost Report*—'I am upper class so I look down on him . . .' etc.

In January 2002 Evelyn Waugh's granddaughter published a novel, *The New You Survival Kit*. In a commentary she suggests that 'the old upper class surrendered its pleasant position in this country a long time ago. In fact the old upper class are little more than our punch bags now, the only ethnic minority everyone is allowed to jeer at . . . The majority of old Us have either added a useful estuary twang to their accents, denied any connection with their roots and previous advantages and joined the job market, or retired to the country for good.'

Ms Waugh discovers a vacuum and promptly fills it with headline hugging members of the fashionable glitterati:

> With their unified revulsion at the old system, their casual clothes, their humorous, ironic 'takes', their social consciences, their insistence that the post boy and the cleaner call them 'Derek' it would be very hard to resent our new leaders very much.

But Ms Waugh smells a rat:

> In fact I am reeling from the smell of it . . . Our new meritoratic elite—the New U (the New You perhaps) may not differentiate, as the old U did, between people who say 'toi-

let' or 'serviette' but we shouldn't be fooled. Its members' code is every bit as snobbish.

However, Ms Waugh appears to capitulate to the barbarians in a way which would shock and disappoint her grandfather and her father.

I am the New U's vanquished foe and for the sake of survival (like many old U's) or perhaps more honestly for the sake of my own ambitions (because privilege is not a pleasant thing to give up), I have tried to learn from the mannerisms of my superiors. I have toned down my upper class accent, and I force myself to read the *Guardian* once a week. Know thy enemy, we are told. I have studied them obsessively . . .

She finds that her surrender pays handsome dividends:

By now my career—and my finances—have picked up. I too can shop at Agnes B and often do. I can enjoy yoga classes at Holmes Place. I can say I'm busy. I can talk at length and with cutting irony about whether Robbie and Nicole are getting it on. I can sound appropriately troubled when the anti-Muslim groundswell is referred to. I can pretend to get the point of the Turner prize. I can look excited at the thought of eating zucchini flowers. Yes, I can!

She rises to a spirited peroration.

The fact is tie or no tie, call him Derek or call him m'Lord, this new ruling class is just like any other. If the New You's weren't so bloody prissy and bourgeois and hypocritical they—I mean we—might even dare to admit it. And then, God bless us, we might even start having some fun.

But surely nothing as daring as a tease?

Ned Sherrin
March 2002

Source Acknowledgements

Material quoted in the Introduction has been taken from the following sources. The Publishers are grateful to the relevant copyright holders for permission to include such material.

The Letters of Nancy Mitford: Love from Nancy, edited by Charlotte Mosley (Hodder & Stoughton, 1993). Copyright © Charlotte Mosley 1993.

Nancy Mitford, Selina Hastings (Hamish Hamilton Ltd, 1985). Copyright © Selina Hastings 1985.

Nancy Mitford: A Memoir, Harold Acton (Hamish Hamilton, 1975). Copyright © Sir Harold Acton 1975.

The Pursuit of Love: A Novel, Nancy Mitford (Penguin in association with Hamish Hamilton Ltd, 1945). Copyright © Nancy Mitford 1945.

A Fine Old Conflict, Jessica Mitford (Michael Joseph, 1977). Copyright © Jessica Mitford 1977.

The Letters of Evelyn Waugh, edited by Mark Amory (Weidenfeld and Nicholson, 1980). Copyright in the letters © The Estate of Laura Waugh 1980.

The Diaries of Evelyn Waugh, edited by Michael Davie (Weidenfeld and Nicholson, 1976). Copyright © The Estate of Evelyn Waugh 1976.

The New Survival Kit, Daisy Waugh (Harper Collins, 2002). Copyright © Daisy Waugh 2002.

'M.S. Found Under a Serviette in a Lovely Home', pp. 456–7 in *Collected Verse from 1929 On* (J. M. Dent & Sons Ltd, 1961). Copyright © Curtis Brown. First Published in *The New Yorker* September 1956.

U AND NON-U

AN ESSAY IN SOCIOLOGICAL LINGUISTICS

by

ALAN S. C. ROSS

U AND NON-U
AN *ESSAY IN SOCIOLOGICAL LINGUISTICS*

TODAY, in 1956, the English class-system is essentially tripartite—there exist an upper, a middle, and a lower class. It is solely by its language that the upper class is clearly marked off from the others. In times past (e.g. in the Victorian and Edwardian periods) this was not the case. But, today, a member of the upper class is, for instance, not necessarily better educated, cleaner, or richer than someone not of this class. Nor, in general, is he likely to play a greater part in public affairs, be supported by other trades or professions,[1] or engage in other pursuits or pastimes than his fellow of another class. There are, it is true, still a few minor points of life which may serve to demarcate the upper class,[2] but they are

[1] It may, however, be doubted how far the Navy and the Diplomatic Service will in practice (in contradistinction to theory) be 'democratized', even if there should be a succession of Labour Governments; foreigners seem to expect English diplomats to be of the upper class.

[2] In this article I use the terms *upper class* (abbreviated: U), *correct, proper, legitimate, appropriate* (sometimes also *possible*) and similar expressions (including some containing the word *should*) to designate usages of the upper class; their antonyms

only minor ones. The games of real tennis and piquet,[1] an aversion to high tea, having one's cards[2] engraved

(non-U, incorrect, not proper, not legitimate, etc.) to designate usages which are not upper class. These terms are, of course, used factually and not in reprobation (indeed I may at this juncture emphasize a point which is doubtless obvious, namely that this whole article is purely factual). *Normal* means common both to U and non-U. I often use expressions such as *U-speaker* to denote a member of the upper class and, also, *gentleman,* pl. *gentlemen* (for brevity, in respect of either sex —the plural *gentlefolk* is no longer U). Class-distinction is very dear to the heart of the upper class and talk about it is hedged with taboo. Hence, as in sexual matters, a large number of circumlocutions is used. Forty years ago, as I understand, U-speakers made use of *lady* and *gentleman* without self-consciousness; the antonym of *gentleman* was often *cad* or *bounder.* Today, save by older people, these terms can hardly be used to indicate class-distinction, for they sound either pedantic or facetious *(you cad, Sir!). Lady* and *gentleman* have, of course, senses quite unconnected with class-distinction, but, today, the use of these words in the senses 'man' and 'woman' between U-speakers has almost entirely vanished save when prefixed with *old (There's an old LADY to see you* is different from *There's an old WOMAN to see you,* for the former implies that the person is U, the latter that she is very non-U). *She's a nice lady* is non-U, *He's a nice gentleman* even more so *(man, woman,* or *girl* being the U-use here).

[1] But solo whist (or *solo* as its devotees call it) is non-U, though much 'lower' games (e.g. pontoon, nap, and even Slippery Sam) are not necessarily so. Whist used to be a U-game but is, today, almost entirely confined to whist-drives, which are non-U *(they STAND UP to deal, my dear!).*

[2] The normal U-word is *card* (though this is ambiguous with

(not printed), not playing tennis in braces, and, in some cases, a dislike of certain comparatively modern inventions such as the telephone, the cinema, and the wireless, are still perhaps marks of the upper class.[1] Again, when drunk, gentlemen often become amorous or maudlin or vomit in public, but they never become truculent.

In the present article I am concerned with the linguistic demarcation of the upper class. This subject has been but little investigated, though it is much discussed, in an unscientific manner, by members of that class. The late Professor H. C. Wyld wrote a short article on the subject. He was well equipped for the task, for he was both a gentleman and a philologist. Today, his views are perhaps a little old-fashioned; for instance, the dictum 'No gentleman goes on a bus', attributed to him, is one which most gentlemen have to neglect.

Both the written and the spoken language of the upper class serve to demarcate it, but the former to only a very

---

(playing)-card). *Carte de visite* was apparently U but would today seem unbearably old-fashioned. *Calling-card* and *visiting-card* are non-U; the latter term is, in any case, an unfortunate one because of the non-U slang phrase *He's left his visiting-card* (of a dog) — foreigners would do well to beware of 'idiomatic' sentences such as *The Picts left their visiting-card in the Pentland Firth* (said, in a public lecture, meaning that the name *Pict* is preserved in the first element of *Pentland*).

[1]Certainly many U-speakers hunt — but hunting has for long been something that the *nouveau riche* knows he should do in order to be U; many farmers hunt too. So, today, hunting is not *ipso facto* a class-indicator.

slight extent. A piece of mathematics or a novel written by a member of the upper class is not likely to differ in any way from one written by a member of another class, except in so far as the novel contains conversation. In writing, it is, in fact, only modes of address, postal addresses, and habits of beginning and ending letters that serve to demarcate the class.

Before proceeding to the detail of the present study I must emphasize that I am here concerned only with usages which serve to demarcate the upper class. The line of demarcation relevant to this study is, often, a line between, on the one hand, gentlemen and, on the other, persons who, though not gentlemen, might at first sight appear, or would wish to appear, as such. Thus, habits of speech peculiar to the lower classes find no place here. I may also note here that the U-demarcation is of two types: (1) a certain U-feature has a different, non-U, counterpart, as non-U *wealthy* = U *rich*; (2) a certain feature is confined to U-speech and it has a counterpart which is not confined to non-U speech, e.g. the pronunciations of *girl* to rhyme with *hell* and *Hal* are U, but many (perhaps most male) U-speakers, like all non-U-speakers, use the pronunciation that rhymes with *curl*.

I. *The Written Language*

The following points may be considered:
(1) Names on envelopes, etc.
(2) Beginnings of letters.
(3) Names on cards.

(4) Postal addresses on envelopes, etc., at the heads of letters, and on cards.

(5) Letter—endings.

Of these points the first three are mutually linked and the second —beginnings of letters —is linked with the spoken language; for, in general, a person known to the writer is written to and spoken to in the same mode of address. It will therefore be convenient to treat all modes of address together, though this means taking the spoken modes out of place.

Modes of address, particularly those used for the nobility, have always been a bugbear to the non-U. It is, for instance, non-U to speak of an earl as *The Earl of P*—; he should be spoken of and to as *Lord P* — and also so addressed at the beginning of a letter if an introduction between him and the speaker/writer has been effected. If the acquaintance is close, *P*— should be used instead of *Lord P* —. Letters to baronets and knights to whom one has been introduced should begin *Dear Sir A* — X —[1] if the acquaintance is slight, *Dear Sir A* — if it is not slight. In speaking *to* one, only *Sir A* — is possible. In speaking *of* one, *Sir A* — should not be used unless the acquaintance is fairly close, *Sir A* — X—, or X —, being correct. If the acquaintance is slight or non-existent, the use of *Sir A* — in speaking of a baronet or knight is non-U and 'snobbish'[2] as attempting to raise the social tone of the speaker.

---

[1] *A*—, *B* —, *C*—, etc. are christian names (the initials being written *A., B., C.,* etc.); X— is a surname.

[2] 'Snobs' are of two kinds; *true snobs* (Thackeray's kind) and *inverted snobs*. Both kinds respect a person the more the better

Should be addressed H.E.

Letters to ambassadors whom one does not know should begin *Dear Excellency* and the envelope should be addressed *H.E. The P— Ambassador.* In speech, a Lieutenant-Commander is addressed as *Commander*, a Lieutenant in the Army as *Mister.* In concluding this section it may be noted that, in writing letters to noblemen of very high rank, the rules laid down in the etiquette-books[1] need not always be strictly observed. Thus a Duke addressed by a stranger as *Dear Sir* would not necessarily conclude that his correspondent was non-U; he might be a left-wing gentleman with a dislike of dukedoms.

On envelopes, gentlemen put *Esq.* after the names of persons who are, or who might wish to be considered, gentlemen, whether in fact armigerous or not. *Esq.* is, however, not used of oneself, e.g. neither on a card (which bears *Mr.)* nor on a stamped-and-addressed envelope

bred he is. True snobs indicate this in their behaviour to, and in their conversation about, persons of good family, though they do not usually admit this. In their conversation about (but not in their behaviour to) such persons, inverted snobs indicate that they respect a person the less the better bred he is. One would expect to find a third category: those who really do respect a person the less the better bred he is, and indicate it. But this third category does not appear to exist. Nearly all English people are snobs of one of the two kinds (in this respect England differs from Finland and Iceland and resembles Spain and pre-War Hungary). And, just as it is impossible to find someone exactly half male and half female, so it is impossible to find an Englishman in whom true and inverted snobbery exactly balance.

[1] It is, of course, very non-U actually to consult these.

enclosed for a reply (which has merely *A —B. X —* or *A. B. X —* without prefix). Knowledge of at least one initial of the recipient's name is, of course, a prerequisite for addressing him with *Esq.* If the writer has not this minimum knowledge (and cannot, or is too lazy to obtain it) he will be in a quandary. In these circumstances I myself use the Greek letter θ (as θ. *Smith, Esq.),* but this is probably idiosyncratic. But to address someone as ' —*Smith', Esq.* is not so much non-U as definitely rude.[1] Gentlemen usually address non-U males as *Mr.*; in internal circulation (e.g. in Government offices), gentlemen may address each other in this way. Schoolboys at their preparatory school (and younger boys) should be addressed as *Master;* at their public school, merely as *A. B. X—* (without prefix or suffix). The non-U usually address all adult males as *Mr.,* but tradespeople have copied the use of *Esq.* from their customers. Those gentlemen who are inverted snobs dislike *Esq.,* but, since they know that to address someone as *Mr.* is non-U, they avoid this also and address all adult males without prefix or suffix (like the correct mode of address for public-schoolboys). Intellectuals, of any class, often begin letters, even where the acquaintance is slight, *with Dear A— X—.*

Postal addresses. It is non-U to place the name of a house in inverted commas (as *"Fairmeads")* or to write the number in full, either without or (especially) with inverted commas (as *Two, —*worse *"Two", —St. Patrick's Avenue).*

---

[1] I may note here that many U-speakers omit the *Esq.* on cheques.

The names of many houses are themselves non-U; the ideal U-address is *P— Q —, R —*, where *P —* is a place-name, *Q —* a describer, and *R —*the name (or abbreviation) of a county as *Shinwell Hall, Salop*.[1] But, today, few gentlemen can maintain this standard and they often live in houses with non-U names such as *Fairmeads* or *El Nido*.

Letter-endings. The U-rules for ending letters are very strict; failure to observe them usually implies non-U-ness, sometimes only youth. In general, the endings of letters are conditioned by their beginnings. Thus a beginning *(Dear) Sir*[2] requires the ending *Yours faithfully*, unless the writer hopes to meet the recipient when *Yours very truly* may be used. Acquaintances who begin letters with *Dear Mr. X —* sign them *Yours sincerely* or *Yours very sincerely*; perversely, the latter ending is less cordial than the former. People who know each other really well will begin *Dear A —* or *Dear X—* (males only) and sign *Yours ever*. The ending *Yours* is often used even by gentlemen if they are in doubt as to which ending is appropriate.

The name after the letter-ending offers little scope for comment. Letters are perhaps most usually signed in such

[1] Here I may note a curious indicator. In speaking, it is, in general, non-U to use the whole name of such a house as in *I'm going to Shinwell Hall* (the U-sentence would be *I'm going to Shinwell*) —this obtains whether the house belongs to the speaker (or his relatives) or not.

[2] Whether the writer is U or not, this is the normal beginning of all business letters to unknowns, the variant *Sir* is correctly used to Government officials, *Sire* (or *Your Majesty*) to kings; *My Dear Sir* is felt as American.

forms as A — X —, A — B. X—, A. B — X— (the choice between the two last depending upon which christian name the writer is normally called by). If the writer is unknown (or not well known) to the recipient, the latter cannot know whether the former is plain *Mr.* (if male), *Miss, Mrs.,* or something else (if female); it is therefore usual for the writer to inform the recipient if he is other than plain *Mr.* (if male), other than *Miss* (if female). In handwritten letters, a usual way of doing this is to sign as, for instance, *(Professor)* A — B. *X* —; in typewritten letters *(Professor* A — B. *X—)* may be typed below the handwritten signature A — B. *X* —. I have seen long titles (e.g. *Dowager Countess of)* appended as footnotes to the signature. In concluding this section I may mention that people sometimes sign themselves (or enter their names in lists, etc.) with the surname only; this usage is very non-U, the reason for its non-U-ness lying in the fact that the correct signature of peers is of this form (e.g. the Earl of P — signs himself just *P—).*[1]

Here I may refer to R. W. Chapman's excellent *Names, designations & appellations,* published in 1946.[2] The author states (p. 231) that the work is 'an attempt to describe the modern use, in good society in this country, of personal

---

[1] The correct form of postcards differs slightly from that of letters, for both the beginning *(Dear* A —, etc.) and the ending *(Yours sincerely,* etc.) are omitted. Some U—speakers feel it wrong to sign a postcard to a friend by anything save the bare initial(s) (A. or A. *B. X.).*

[2] S P. E. Tract No. XLVII.

names and designations, spoken or written, in the second or third person'.¹ Chapman does not specifically deal with non-U usages but, since his enumeration is intended as exhaustive, it may be assumed that, essentially, usages divergent from those given by him are non-U, except in so far as I have dealt with them.

I may comment on certain points mentioned by Chapman where the usage of 1956 differs from that of a rather old-fashioned person writing some years earlier. I arrange the commentary by the pages of his book, either citing passages therefrom in inverted commas, or (where this would be too lengthy) indicating in square brackets [' '] the point under discussion.

pp. 237–8. ['Spouse: third person.'] The mode in which a speaker refers to his spouse is markedly distinct as between U- and non-U-speakers. A U-speaker, naming his wife to an equal, normally says *My wife* (or uses her christian name); to a very non-U person he says *Mrs. X—*. Chapman says (p. 237) of a U-speaker referring to the hearer's wife [' " Your wife" may be over-familiar if I do not know Jones (i.e. the hearer) very well']. He advocates the use, then, of *Mrs. Jones.* Actually, I think that, of recent years, there has been a considerable increase in the use of *Your wife, Your husband* by U-speakers, even in cases where the acquaintance is of the slightest. Non-U-speakers do not in general make use of *my/your wife/husband*, preferring *Mr./Mrs. X—*.

---

¹ By the 'second person' he means speaking *to* a person, by the 'third person', speaking *of* one.

p. 238. [" What does Weston think of the weather?",
Mr. Knightly asked Mrs. Weston. But I should be chary
of following this precedent.'] I agree with Chapman.
There is, however, rather a similar case, not mentioned by
Chapman (doubtless because it is a very minor one),
where surnames may be used. Schoolboys and young men
frequently refer to each other by their surnames, so parents of a boy, talking to one of his acquaintances, often use
the acquaintance's surname because they do not know his
christian name; similarly, the acquaintance may call the
son by his surname to the parents. It is not until a boy
gets older (c. 16?) that he realizes that he must deliberately ascertain his friends' christian names in order to be
able to refer to them correctly to their parents. At Oxford
in the late twenties the use of the surname in these circumstances was a known *gaucherie* and must therefore
have been fairly usual.[1]

p. 240. [" Sir" is, of course, very often used between
intimates with a slightly jocular or affectionate intention;
one may say "Good morning, Sir" to almost any intimate.
"My dear Sir, I am very glad to see you." But "My dear
Sir" usually conveys a mild remonstrance'.] These usages

[1] In connection with surnames, I may mention a habit not
noted by Chapman, viz. the abbreviation of the surnames of
close friends. It was apparently U and was certainly thriving in
the nineties; at a much earlier period it appears in Mrs. Henry
Wood's *Johnny Ludlow* where the young *Todhetley* is often
called *Tod.* The custom is now obsolescent, save perhaps in the
case of hyphenated surnames *(X-Y* may be called *X)* and
between close women-friends (e.g. a *Miss Robinson* might be
called *Robbie).*

are, I think, obsolescent among U-speakers and young U-speakers are inclined to dislike them very much. In my experience people who use them are either non-U (very often, commercial travellers) or, if U, are elderly academics.

p. 241. ⌈'The use of *"Sir"* by young men to their seniors in general is not easily defined, and the practice varies.'⌉ This is certainly true; my own use is to reserve *Sir* for men of great age and/or great distinction. The War of 1939–45, like its predecessor of 1914–18, has brought about an enormous increase in the use of *Sir* because of Service rules. Chapman says ⌈'Young women . . . are not expected to say *sir'*⌉ —but now many do by reason of their having been in one of the women's Services.

p. 241. ⌈'But is there any alternative (i.e. to *Miss*) if one is addressing a telephone operator or a barmaid?'⌉ Yes, there is: silence, perhaps the most favourite of all U-usages today. Indeed it is remarkable how easy it is (save when engaged in activities such as bridge or poker) to avoid the use of any appellation at all.[1] This has become increasingly the practice of shyer gentlemen. The use of *Miss* in the circumstances mentioned by Chapman

---

[1] This U-habit of silence has had a curious corollary. Most nations say something when drinking (as *Skål!* in Swedish or *Egészségére!* in Hungarian) but, until 1939, English U-speakers normally said nothing. Since then, however, the Service habit of saying something has become almost universal and most U-speakers therefore feel it churlish to say nothing; repressing a shudder, they probably say *Cheers!* (though hardly *God bless!* which, though also frequent in the Services, seems non-U).

(and particularly to waitresses) is definitely non-U.

p. 243. ['Christian names.'] On this matter, Chapman has a point of view out of date even by the early thirties. I can only just remember the time, in the very early twenties, when a typical boy-and-girl conversation might have run: '*He:* May I call you by your christian name? *She:* If you like. *He:* Er —what *is* your christian name?' Since that time the use of christian names by U-speakers has been continually increasing. In the thirties, it was quite customary for a member of a *partie carée* going to a dance who was unknown to the other three to be introduced by the christian name alone (or, often, just as *John Smith* or *Jane Smith*, without prefix). In the War the use of christian names increased still further; in Government offices it was often the custom for a man at the head of a large section of girls to call them all by their christian names, while they called him *Mr.* X —.

p. 248. ['Use of surnames by women.'] In the third person, it is now very usual for women to use the surname only of men (e.g. of their husbands' friends); for men, or women, to use the surnames only of women in this way is less common, though in some circles (e.g. university ones) it is quite accepted. In the second person, the use of the bare surname without Christian name or prefix is rarer still. For a woman so to call a man is still either foreign, bohemian, or intellectual-left. In general, women call other women by the bare surname only in institutions for women (e.g. in girls' schools, women's colleges, hospitals, and, no doubt, in women's prisons).

p. 250. ⌜'Dukes: third person'⌝ I may add that dukes, if fairly well known to the speaker, may appropriately be referred to by christian name and title, e.g. *George Birmingham*, meaning *George, etc., Duke of Birmingham*.

p. 251. ⌜'A facetious use.'⌝ *His Lordship*, in facetious use, is definitely non-U and, often, inverted snob. There is a somewhat similar non-U expression: *young master* (as in *Young master's making himself quite at home!*) used of a young man considered 'la-di-da' (for this word see below).

pp. 251, 255. ⌜'Abbreviations.'⌝ *Honourable* and *Reverend* are abbreviated either as *Honble., Revd.* or as *Hon., Rev.* Both usages are quite U, though the former is the more old-fashioned.

p. 265. ⌜'Some people say "Miss Austen".'⌝ In my experience, to say *Miss Austen* instead of *Jane Austen* is either precious or pseudo-intellectual.

II. *The Spoken Language*

PRONUNCIATION

(1) In a few cases, a difference of stress serves to demarcate a pronunciation as between U and non-U. *Thus yésterdáy* (with the same stress as *Wéstern Ísles*) is non-U as against U *yésterday;* or, again, U *témporarily/* non-U *temporárily;* U *fórmidable/*non-U *formídable;* U *ínt'resting* non-U *interésting; Víenna* is old-fashioned U for normal *Viénna; cónfessor* and *súccessor* (like *Mass* to rhyme with pass, instead of *gas)* appear to be confined to Catholic U-speakers (these call themselves *Catholic* with first syllable to rhyme with *bath).* In some cases two stress-variants may

both be U as *spónge-cake* or *spónge-cáke* (non-U-speakers hardly use the word, substituting *sponge* for it).

(2) To pronounce words like *ride* as if spelt *raid* is non-U *(raid* was, however, undoubtedly Shakespeare's pronunciation of *ride).* This kind of pronunciation is often called *refained.*

(3) Many (but not all) U-speakers make *get* rhyme with *bit, just* (adverb) with *best, catch* with *fetch.*

(4) In U speech, *spoon* rhymes with *boon,* in non-U speech with the Yorkshire pronunciation of *bun.* Some U-speakers make *gone* rhyme with *born.*

(5) U-speakers do not sound the *l* in *golf, Ralph* (which rhymes with *safe), solder;* some old-fashioned *U*-speakers do not sound it in *falcon, Malvern,* either, but it is doubtful how far this last survives.

(6) *Real, ideal* have two, respectively, three syllables in U speech, one, respectively, two in non-U speech (note, especially, non-U *really,* rhyming with *mealie).*

(7) *Fault, also, Balkans, Baltic, halt, malt, salt, vault* are pronounced by the U as if spelt *fawlt, awlso, bawlkans,* etc.

(8) In *Berkeley, Berkshire, clerk, Derby,* U-speakers rhyme the first syllable with. *dark* (or *bar),* non-U speakers with *mirk* (or *burr).*[1]

---

[1] Since it is definitely non-U to pronounce *Berkeley* with first syllable rhyming with *mirk,* U-speakers get a frisson if they have to enunciate the surnames *Birkley, Burkly* (correctly pronounced with *first* syllable rhyming with *mirk)* for, if a U-hearer does not appreciate the spelling of the names (rare ones), they may be suspected of using a non-U pronunciation.

(9) Some U-speakers pronounce *tyre* and *tar* identically (and so for many other words, such as *fire* —even going to the length of making *lion* rhyme with *barn*).

(10) *Miscellaneous words. (a) Acknowledge:* U —rhymes with *college*/non-U —2nd syllable rhymes with *bowl*. *(b) Either:* U — 1st syllable rhymes with *buy*/non-U — 1st syllable rhymes with *bee*. *(c) Forehead:* U —rhymes with *torrid*/non-U —*fore-head*. *(d) Handkerchief:* U —last syllable rhymes with stiff/non-U —last syllable rhymes with *beef* or *weave*. *(e) Hotel* and *humour:* to drop the *h* is old-fashioned U. *(f) Medicine* and *Venison:* U —two syllables/non-U —three syllables. *(g)* U *a nought/* non-U *an ought* (meaning 'zero'). *(h) Tortoise:* U— pronounced identically with *taught us*/non-U —last syllable rhymes with *boys* or *Boyce*. *(i) Vase:* U —rhymes with *bars*/non-U — rhymes with *cause* or *maize*. (j) *W* (the letter):[1] U *double-you*/non-U *dubby-you.*[2]

---

[1] *The W* is a frequent non-U expression for 'the lavatory' *(W.C.* is also non-U) —hence, no doubt, the non-U children's word *dubby or dub.* (In this connection I may mention a *U* expression: *Let me show you the GEOGRAPHY* of *the house* (meaning, essentially 'the lavatory').)

[2] Oddly enough, *Grammar* and *Syntax* (two very important philological domains) produce hardly any marks of class-difference. I have noticed only (i) *I bought it at Woolworth* (without the final *'s),* a usage confined to some U-speakers; (ii) the non-U use of the prepositions in *He's AT boarding-school, She's ON holiday;* (iii) the North Country inversion in *He's been very decent, has John.*

VOCABULARY

Article (meaning 'chamber-pot') is non-U; in so far as the thing survives, U-speakers use *jerry* (a schoolboy term) or *pot*.[1]

Bath. To TAKE a bath is non-U against U *to HAVE one's bath*.

Civil: this word is used by U-speakers to approve the behaviour of a non-U person in that the latter has appreciated the difference between U and non-U, e.g. *The guard was certainly very civil*.

Coach (meaning 'char-à-banc') is non-U, doubtless because the thing itself is. Those U-speakers who are forced, by penury, to use them call them *buses,* thereby causing great confusion (a *coach* runs into the country, a *bus* within a town).

non-U *corsets*/U *stays*.

Counterpane, bedspread, coverlet. Of these three synonyms, I think that the first is U, the second obsolete, the third non-U.

Cruet. The sentence *Pass the cruet, please* is very non-U; *cruets* are in themselves non-U. In gentlemen's houses there are, ideally, separate containers—*salt-cellars, pepper-pots (-castors, -grinders,-mills)* and *mustard-pots*, so that the corresponding U-expression will be *I wonder if you could pass the salt (pepper, mustard), please?* or the like. Vinegar is a fourth constituent of many cruets but many uses of vinegar (e.g. poured on fish or bacon-and-eggs) are definitely non-U.

---

[1] But the (recent?) transitive verb *to pot*, used of babies, is surely non-U?

Crust or crumb? used when cutting bread is (old-fashioned?) non-U.

Cultivated in *They're cultivated people* is non-U and so also is *cultured*. There is really no U-equivalent (some U-speakers use *civilized* in this sense).

Cup. How is your cup? is a non-U equivalent of *Have some more tea?* or the like. Possible negative non-U answers are *I'm doing nicely, thank you* and *(Quite) sufficient, thank you.* There is a well-known non-U affirmative answer: *I don't mind if I do* (but this was U about a century ago).

Cycle is non-U against U *bike, bicycle* (whether verb or noun); non-U *motorcycle*/U *motorbike, motorbicycle* is perhaps less pronouncedly so.

Dinner. U-speakers eat *lunch* in the middle of the day *(luncheon* is old-fashioned U) and *dinner* in the evening; if a U-speaker feels that what he is eating is a travesty of his dinner, he may appropriately call it *supper.* Non-U-speakers (also U-children and U-dogs), on the other hand, have their *dinner* in the middle of the day. *Evening meal* is non-U.

Dress-suit. This is a non-U word. A male U-speaker might answer the question *What shall I wear tonight?* in any of the following ways: (1) *Dinner jacket;* (2) *Short coat* (?old-fashioned); (3) *Black tie;* (4) *Tails;* (5) *White tie.* The term *evening dress* is often used on invitations but it has not a very wide currency among U-speakers (in any case, for men it is ambiguous); a sentence *Shall we wear evening dress?* would not be possible, the appropriate expression being *Are we going to change?*

Excuse my glove. This expression, used when shaking hands, is (?old-fashioned) non-U; male U-speakers do (used to?) remove their glove in order to shake hands but say nothing.

Greatcoat (also *topcoat?*) are rather old-fashioned U, *overcoat* being normal. *Burberry*[1] and *raincoat* are of the same genre, *macintosh* or *mac* being normal.

Greens meaning 'vegetables' is non-U.

Home: non-U *They've a lovely home*/U *They've a very nice house.*

Horse-riding is non-U against U *riding*. From the non-U point of view the expression is reasonable, for to the non-U there are other kinds of riding (cf. non-U *to go for a motor-ride*/U *to go for a drive in a motor-car*). But *bicycle-ride* is normal.

Ill in *I was very ill on the boat* is non-U against U *sick*.

Jack. At cards, *jack* is non-U against U *knave*, save in *jackpot* (at poker). My son, A. W. P. Ross, kindly calls my attention to the following passage from *Great Expectations* (ed. of 1861, vol. I, p. 126): '"He calls the knaves, Jacks, this boy!" said Estella with disdain.'

La-di-da is an expression with which the non-U stigmatize a U habit, speech-habit, or person.

Lounge is a name given by the non-U to a room in their houses; for U-speakers, *hall* or *dining-room* might well be the nearest equivalent (but all speakers, of course, speak of the *lounge* of a hotel).

---

[1] This use of *Burberry* no doubt arose because, even before 1914 (when U-speakers were richer than non-U-speakers), this was a good and expensive kind of macintosh.

non-U *mental*/U *mad.*

A *matter of business* is non-U (as in *Say you've come to see him on a matter of business*).

Mention: If you don't mind my mentioning it is non-U.

Mirror (save in compounds such as *driving-, shaving-mirror*) is non-U against U *looking-glass.*

non-U *note-paper*/U *writing-paper.*[1]

Pardon! is used by the non-U in three main ways: (1) if the hearer does not hear the speaker properly; (2) as an apology (e.g. on brushing by someone in a passage); (3) after hiccupping or belching. The normal U-correspondences are very curt, viz. (1) *What?* (2) *Sorry!* (3) [Silence], though, in the first two cases, U-parents and U-governesses are always trying to make children say something 'politer' — *What did you say?* and *I'm frightfully sorry* are certainly possible. For Case 3 there are other non-U possibilities, e.g. *Manners! Beg Pardon! Pardon me!*

To Pass a (nasty) remark. He passed the remark that . . . is non-U.

Pleased to meet you! This is a very frequent non-U response to the greeting *How d'you do?* U-speakers normally just repeat the greeting; to reply to the greeting (e.g. with *Quite well, thank you)* is non-U.

Posh 'smart' is essentially non-U but, recently, it has gained ground among schoolboys of all classes.

non-U *preserve*/U *jam.*

[1] This distinction (as well as some others, e.g. non-U *perfume*/U *scent)* is noted by Miss Nancy Mitford, *The Pursuit of Love (*1945 ed., p. 31).

non-U *radio*/U *wireless* (but *radio* technically as in air-craft) .

Rude meaning 'indecent' is non-U; there is no universal U-correspondent.

non-U *serviette*/U *table-napkin*; perhaps the best known of all the linguistic class-indicators of English.

Study in *He's studying for an exam*, is definitely non-U (U: *working for*).

Teacher is essentially *non-U*, though *school-teacher* is used by the *U* to indicate a non-U teacher. The U equivalent is *master*, *mistress* with prefixed attribute (as *maths-mistress*). Non-U children often refer to their teachers without article (as, *Teacher says* . . .).

non-U *toilet-paper*/U *lavatory-paper*.

non-U *wealthy*/U *rich*.

Before concluding with some general remarks, there are two points which may appropriately receive mention here.

First, *slang*. There seems no doubt that, in the nineties and at least up to 1914, U-speakers (particularly young ones) were rather addicted to slang. Today, however, U-speakers use it little and regard much use of it as non-U —save, of course, in special circumstances (e.g. in the case of young boys at school). American slang is especially deprecated (save, perhaps, for *O.K.).* The ultimate War, like the penultimate one, brought a flood of slang into the Services, some of it a very vivid kind as, for instance, R.A.F. slang *He tore me off a strip* meaning 'he repri-manded me severely', *I was shot down in flames* meaning 'I was completely overwhelmed in the argument'. Since the War, there has been an unfortunate tendency for non-Service personnel to use Service slang and it is clear that Service personnel regard such use as in very poor taste. Nevertheless, the expressions *I've had it!* (meaning, essentially, 'I have *not* had it') and *That's a bad show,* have become very frequent among all classes of speakers.

Secondly, *changing one's voice.*[1] In England today—just as much as in the England of many years ago—the question 'Can a non-U speaker become a U speaker?'[2] is one noticeably of paramount importance for many Englishmen (and for some of their wives). The answer is that an adult can never attain complete success. Moreover, it must be remembered that, in these matters, U-speakers have ears to hear, so that one single pronunciation, word, or phrase will suffice to brand an apparent U-speaker as originally non-U (for U-speakers themselves never make 'mistakes'). Under these circumstances, efforts to change voice are surely better abandoned. But, in fact, they continue in full force and in all strata of society. On the whole, the effect is deleterious. Thus, to take only one example: in village schools, any natural dialect

[1] This phrase is my own coinage (of many years ago); I know of no other expression.

[2] Logically, the converse question 'Can a U-speaker become a non-U-speaker?' should also arise, but, in practice, it seems not to—even the staunchest of inverted snobs apparently draws the line here. At all events I have only come across one case of it (in Leeds).

that is still left to the children will have superimposed upon it the language of the primary school-teacher (a class of people entirely non-U) so that the children leave school speaking a mixture which has nothing to recommend it. In concluding this paragraph, I may mention that there is one method of effecting change of voice, provided the speaker is young enough. This is, to send him[1] first to a preparatory school, then to a good public-school. This method is one that has been approved for more than a century and, at the moment, it is almost completely effective. It is interesting to speculate upon the state of affairs which will arise when the day comes when virtually no U-speaker will be able to afford to educate his children at these kinds of schools (this day has already dawned).

If we consider the wider implications of the linguistic class-indication discussed above, two points immediately arise: the linguistic class—indicators are almost all philologically trivial and, apparently, almost all of a very ephemeral nature. I am convinced that a thorough historical study of the class-indicators discussed above would reveal many present-day U-features as non-U at an earlier period and vice versa. To take an example. In his *Critical pronouncing dictionary and expositor of the English language,* published in 1791, J. Walker is clearly trying to differentiate between U and non-U usage. Yet nearly all the points mentioned by him—only one hundred and sixty years ago—are now 'dead' and with-out class-

---

[1] Today similar arrangements can be made for girls; the older approved method was, of course, a U-governess.

significance, in that one of the pronunciations given is today no longer known in any kind of English save dialect. Only one of Walker's U indicators *(-in'* of *huntin', shootin', and fishin')* is so recognized by me and even that one I regard as belonging to an era earlier than my own. In two cases of double pronunciations, today's U alternative is chosen by Walker as the non-U one, viz. (I quote) (1) *'Either* and *neither* are . . . often pronounced *eye-ther and nigh-ther.* . . . Analogy, however, without hesitation, gives the diphthong the sound of long *e* and rhymes them with *breather*, one who breathes. This is the pronunciation Mr. Garrick always gave to these words, and which is undoubtedly the true one.' (2) 'The proper names *Derby* and *Berkeley*, still retain the old sound, as if written *Darby* and *Barkeley:* but even these, in polite usage, are getting into the common sound, nearly as if written *Durby* and *Burkeley.'* Walker feels strongly on various matters: 'The vulgar . . . pronounce the *o* obscurely, and sometimes as if followed by *r*, as *winder, feller*, for *window* and *fellow;* but this is almost too despicable for notice'—but the pronunciation of *fellow* fulminated against by Walker is, to me, old-fashioned U (though I make the word rhyme with *bellow* myself).

Among European languages, English is, surely, the one most suited to the study of linguistic class-distinction. I do not really know how far such a thing may exist in others. In Finnish, I have the impression that no phenomena of the sort exist. In German, there may well have been something comparable; certainly, I recall that, in good

Potsdam society of the late twenties, the expression *küss'
die hand* (on introduction to a female) was definitely
frowned on—but this society has vanished without trace.
In present-day Russian, the distinction between the two
plurals of *ofitser* 'officer'—*ofitsery* and *ofitsera*—is certainly
one of class. There seems to be remarkably little literature
on the subject save perhaps (rather naturally) by Russians
and/or as concerns Russian. The position in Russia is
indeed interesting, for, in that country, it is obviously
desirable to speak in a non-U manner rather than in a U
one. (There is an excellent book on the subject, in Russian,
by Zhirmunskii.) It is to be hoped that more studies of linguistic class-distinction in the European languages will
one day be forthcoming.

However the general concept of a certain variant of a
language appertaining to a certain section of its speakers
(e.g. old women, or children) is one very well known to
anthropologists and it is, no doubt, in the African jungle
and among the Red Indians that we shall find the gener-
alized form of the linguistic indicators of our English
class-distinction. This is a suitable point at which to end
this article, for we have now reached that awkward terrain
where Linguistics marches with Anthropology—and the
anthropologists have, alas, not been appreciably active
here.

THE ENGLISH ARISTOCRACY

by

NANCY MITFORD

THE ENGLISH ARISTOCRACY

THE English aristocracy may seem to be on the verge of
decadence, but it is the only real aristocracy left in the
world today. It has real political power through the House
of Lords and a real social position through the Queen. An
aristocracy in a republic is like a chicken whose head has
been cut off: it may run about in a lively way, but in fact it
is dead. There is nothing to stop a Frenchman, German,
or Italian from calling himself the Duke of Carabosse if he
wants to, and in fact the Continent abounds with invented
titles. But in England the Queen is the fountain of hon-
ours and when she bestows a peerage upon a subject she
bestows something real and unique.

The great distinction between the English aristocracy
and any other has always been that, whereas abroad every
member of a noble family is noble, in England none are
noble except the head of the family. In spite of the fact that
they enjoy courtesy titles, the sons and daughters
of lords are commoners—though not so common as
baronets and their wives who take precedence after hon-

*Younger son of an earl taking precedence over Knight of the
Garter*

ourables. (So, of course, do all knights, except Knights of the Garter who come after the eldest sons and the daughters of barons, but before the younger sons.) The descendants of younger sons, who on the Continent would all be counts or barons, in England have no titles and sit even below knights. Furthermore, the younger sons and daughters of the very richest lords receive, by English custom, but little money from their families, barely enough to live on. The sons are given the same education as their eldest brother and then turned out, as soon as they are grown up, to fend for themselves; the daughters are given no education at all, the general idea being that they must find some man to keep them—which, in fact, they usually do. The rule of primogeniture has kept together the huge fortunes of English lords; it has also formed our class system.

There is in England no aristocratic class that forms a caste. We have about 950 peers, not all of whom, incidentally, sit in the House of Lords. Irish peers have no seats, though some Irish peers have a subsidiary U.K. peerage giving a seat; Scotch peers elect sixteen representatives from among themselves. Peeresses in their own right are not, as yet, admitted. Most of the peers share the education, usage, and point of view of a vast upper middle class, but the upper middle class does not, in its turn, merge imperceptibly into the middle class. There is a very definite border line, easily recognizable by hundreds of small but significant landmarks.

When I speak of these matters I am always accused of

being a snob, so, to illustrate my point, I propose to quote from Professor Alan Ross of Birmingham University. Professor Ross has written a paper, printed in Helsinki in 1954 for the *Bulletin de la Société Neo-philologique de Helsinki*, on 'Upper Class English Usage'. Nobody is likely to accuse either this learned man or his Finnish readers of undue snobbishness. The Professor, pointing out that it is solely by their language that the upper classes nowadays are distinguished (since they are neither cleaner, richer, nor better-educated than anybody else), has invented a useful formula: U (for upper class)-speaker versus non-U-speaker. Such exaggeratedly non-U usage as 'serviette' for 'napkin' he calls non-U indicators. Since 'a piece of mathematics or a novel written by a member of the upper class is not likely to differ in any way from one written by a member of another class . . . in writing it is in fact only modes of address, postal addresses and habits of beginning and ending letters that serve to demarcate the class'. . . . The names of many houses are themselves non-U; the ideal U-address is PQR where P is a place-name, Q a describer, and R the name of a county, as 'Shirwell Hall, Salop'. (Here I find myself in disagreement with Professor Ross—in my view abbreviations such as Salop, Herts, or Glos, are decidedly non-U. Any sign of undue haste, in fact, is apt to be non-U, and I go so far as preferring, except for business letters, not to use air mail.) 'But', adds Professor Ross, 'today few gentlemen can maintain this standard and they often live in houses with non-U names such as Fairmeads or El Nido.' Alas!

He speaks of the U-habit of silence, and perhaps does not make as much of it as he might. Silence is the only possible U-response to many embarrassing modern situations: the ejaculation of 'cheers'[1] before drinking, for example, or 'it was so nice seeing you', after saying goodbye. In silence, too, one must endure the use of the Christian name by comparative strangers and the horror of being introduced by Christian and surname without any prefix. This unspeakable usage sometimes occurs in letters —Dear XX —which, in silence, are quickly torn up, by me.

After discoursing at some length on pronunciation, the professor goes on to vocabulary and gives various examples of U and non-U usage.

Cycle is non-U against U *bike.*

Dinner: U-speakers eat *luncheon* in the middle of the day and *dinner* in the evening. Non-U speakers (also U-children and U-dogs) have their *dinner* in the middle of the day.

Greens is non-U for U *vegetables.*

Home: non-U—'they have a lovely *home*'; U—'*they've* a very nice *house*'.

Ill: 'I was *ill* on the boat' is non-U against U *sick.*

Mental: non-U for U *mad.*

Toilet paper: non-U for U *lavatory paper.*

Wealthy: non-U for U *rich.*

To these I would add:

Sweet: non-U for U *pudding.*

---

[1] See Evelyn Waugh, *Men at Arms*, pp. 40, 44. But then Mr. Crouchback is a saint.

Dentures: non-U for U *false teeth*. This, and *glasses* for *spectacles*, almost amount to non-U indicators.

Wire: non-U for U *telegram*.

Britain: non-U for U *England* ('The country which had been lost to view as Britain re-appears as England.' Lord Macaulay.)

Scottish: non-U for U *Scotch*. I have a game I play with all printers. I write Scotch, it appears in the proofs as Scottish. I correct it back to Scotch. About once in three times I get away with it.

Phone, Bye-bye and *Riding* (except a horse or a bicycle) are non-U indicators. The dreadful Bye-bye has been picked up by the French, and one hears them saying *Bon —alors bye-bye mon vieux*. It makes me blush for my country.

(One must add that the issue is sometimes confused by U-speakers using non-U indicators as a joke. Thus Uncle Matthew in *The Pursuit of Love* speaks of his *dentures*.)

Finally Professor Ross poses the question: Can a non-U speaker become a U-speaker? His conclusion is that an adult can never achieve complete success 'because one word or phrase will suffice to brand an apparent U-speaker as originally non-U (for U-speakers themselves never make mistakes)'. I am not quite sure about this. Usage changes very quickly and I even know undisputed U-speakers who pronounce girl 'gurl', which twenty years ago would have been unthinkable. All the same, it is true that one U-speaker recognizes another U-speaker almost as soon as he opens his mouth, though

U-speaker A may deplore certain lapses in the conversation of U-speaker B.

From these U-speakers spring the 'sensible men of substantial means' who, as Bagehot observed in 1875, 'are what we wish to be ruled by' and who still seem to rule our land. When the means of these sensible men become sufficiently ample they can very easily be ennobled, should they wish it, and join the House of Lords. It might therefore be supposed that there is no aristocracy at all in England, merely an upper middle class, some of whom are lords; but, oddly enough, this is not so. A lord does not have to be born to his position and, indeed, can acquire it through political activities, or the sale of such unaristocratic merchandise as beer, but though he may not be a U-speaker he becomes an aristocrat as soon as he receives his title. The Queen turns him from socialist leader, or middle-class businessman, into a nobleman, and his outlook from now on will be the outlook of an aristocrat.

Ancestry has never counted much in England. The English lord knows himself to be such a very genuine article that, when looking for a wife, he can rise above such baubles as seize quartiers. Kind hearts, in his view, are more than coronets, and large tracts of town property more than Norman blood. He marries for love, and is rather inclined to love where money is; he rarely marries in order to improve his coat of arms. (Heiresses have caused the extinction as well as the enrichment of many an English family, since the heiress, who must be an only child if she is to be really rich, often comes of barren or

enfeebled stock.) This unconcern for pedigree leads people
to suppose that the English lords are a jumped-up lot, and
that their families are very seldom 'genuine' and 'old'. One
often hears it said, 'No Englishman alive today would be
eligible to drive in the carriage of a King of France'. '
Nobody really has Norman blood.' 'The true aristocracy
of England was wiped out in the Wars of the Roses.' And
so on.

There is some truth in all these statements, but it is not
the whole truth. Many of our oldest families have never
been ennobled. Some no longer hold peerages. The
ancient Scrope family has, in its time, held the baronies of
Scrope of Marsham and Scrope of Bolton, the earldoms of
Wiltshire and of Sunderland, the sovereignty of the Isle of
Man, but the head of the family is now Mr. Scrope. If he
should be offered a peerage he would no doubt proudly
refuse. The only existing families known to descend from
knights who came over with William the Conqueror in
time to fight at Hastings, the Malets, the Giffards and the
Gresleys and (according to *Burke's Landed Gentry* 1952)
the De Marris, are another case in point. Of the Norman
knights who came during William's reign or later, some
were never anything but country gentlemen, but some are
the direct ancestors of modern peers: St. John, Talbot,
West, Curzon, Clinton, Grey, Seymour, St. Aubyn,
Sinclair, Haig, and Hay, for instance. There are 100 peers
of England from before the Union (including Prince
Charles, as Duke of Cornwall). All of them are descended
in the female line from King Edward III, except possibly
Lord Byron, though a little research would probably find

him an Edward III descent. All peers, except barons, are officially styled 'Cousin' by the Queen; as regards most dukes and earls this is not so much fiction as a distant truth. Only 26 earls have been created in this century and they have all been great men like Lloyd George and Haig. (The Haigs have borne arms and lived at Bemersyde since the 12th century but had never previously been ennobled.)

The dukes are rather new creations. When James I came to the throne there were no dukes at all, the high traitors Norfolk and Somerset having had their dukedoms attainted. They were both restored in 1660. Between 1660 and 1760, 18 dukedoms were created. On the whole, Englishmen are made dukes as a reward for being rich or royal (4 descend from bastards of Charles II), though dukedoms have sometimes been bestowed for merit. The oldest title is that of Earl. Several medieval earldoms still exist. Sixty-five barons hold titles from before 1711. Three hundred and twenty-seven of the present-day peerages were created before 1800, 382 belong to families which have borne arms in the direct male line since before 1485 and which are therefore eligible, as far as birth is concerned, to be Knights of Malta.

But whether their families are 'old' or 'new' is of small account —the lords all have one thing in common: they share an aristocratic attitude to life. What is this attitude? The purpose of the aristocrat is to lead, therefore his functions are military and political. There can be no doubt of the military excellence of our noblemen. Two

hundred and fourteen peers alive today have been deco-
rated in battle or mentioned in despatches. The families
of the premier duke and the premier earl of England hold
the George Cross. In politics, including the unglam-
orous and often boring local politics, they have worked
hard for no reward and done their best according to their
lights.

The purpose of the aristocrat is most emphatically not to
work for money. His ancestors may have worked in order
to amass the fortune which he enjoys, though on the
whole the vast riches of the English lords come from
sources unconnected with honest toil; but he will seldom
do the same. His mind is not occupied with money, it
turns upon other matters. When money is there he spends
it on maintaining himself in his station. When it is no
longer there he ceases to spend, he draws in his horns.
Even the younger sons of lords seem, in all ages, to have
been infected with this point of view: there is nothing so
rare as for the scion of a noble house to make a fortune by
his own efforts. In the old days they went into professions
—the Army, the Navy, diplomacy, and the Church—in
which it is impossible to earn more than a living. Those
who went to the colonies were administrators, they rarely
feathered their nests—the great nabobs were essentially
middle class. Nowadays younger sons go into the City,
but I have yet to hear of one making a large fortune; more
often they lose in unwise speculations what little capital
they happen to own.

All this should not be taken as a sign that our lords are
lazy or unenterprising The point is that, in their view,

effort is unrelated to money. Now this view has, to a large extent, communicated itself to the English race and nation with the result that our outlook is totally different from that of our American cousins, who have never had an aristocracy. Americans relate all effort, all work, and all of life itself to the dollar. Their talk is of nothing but dollars. The English seldom sit happily chatting for hours on end about pounds. In England, public business is its own reward, nobody would go into Parliament in order to become rich, neither do riches bring public appointments. Our ambassadors to foreign states are experienced diplomatists, not socially ambitious million-airesses.

This idiosyncratic view of money has its good side and its bad. Let us glance at the case history of Lord Fortinbras. Fortinbras is ruined—we are now in the 1930's. (All English noblemen, according to themselves, are ruined, a fantasy I shall deal with later, but Fortin-bras really is.) He is not ruined because of death duties, since his father died when he was a child, before they became so heavy, but because he and his forbears have always regarded their estates with the eyes of sportsmen rather than of cultivators. It is useless for him to plead that the policy of cheap corn has been his downfall; an intelligent landowner has always been able to make money with prize cattle, racehorses, market gardens, timber, and so on. But Fortinbras's woods have been looked after by gamekeepers and not by woodmen, his farms have been let to tenants chosen for their tenderness towards foxes and partridges rather than for their agricultural efficiency. His land is undercapitalized, his cot-tagers live in conditions no better than those of their Saxon forbears, water and electric light are laid on in his stables but not in the dwellings of his tenantry. He has made various unwise speculations and lost a 'packet' on the Turf. In short, he deserves to be ruined and he is ruined.

Now what does he do? He is young, healthy, and not stupid; his wife, the daughter of another peer, is hand-some, bossy, and energetic. She is the kind of woman who, in America, would be running something with enormous efficiency and earning thousands. They have two babies, Dominick and Caroline, and a Nanny. Does it occur to either Lord or Lady Fortinbras to get a job and retrieve the family fortunes? It does not. First of all they sell everything that is not entailed, thus staving off actual want. They shut up most of the rooms in their house, send away the servants (except, of course, Nanny), and get the Dowager Lady Fortinbras and her sister to come and cook, clean, dust, and take trays upstairs to the nursery. Old Lady Fortinbras is quite useful, and Lady Enid is a treasure. The Fortinbrases realize that they are very lucky, and if at heart they wish there were a mother's hall for the two ladies to sit in of an evening, they never say so, even to each other. Fortinbras chops the wood, stokes the boiler, brings in the coal, washes the Morris Cowley, and drives off in it to attend the County Council and sit on the Bench. Lady Fortinbras helps in the house, digs in the border, exercises the Border terriers, and also does a great deal of committee work. They are both on the go from morning to night, but it is a go that does not bring in one penny. Their friends and neighbours all say, 'Aren't the Fortinbrases wonderful?'

Comes the war. They clear the decks by sending Nanny and the children to an American couple, the Karamazovs, whom they once met at St. Moritz and who have sent them Christmas cards ever since. Fortinbras goes off with his territorials and Lady Fortinbras joins the A.T.S. Their war records are brilliant in the extreme, their energy, courage, and instinct for leadership have at last found an outlet, and in no time at all they both become generals. After the war they are not surprised to find themselves more ruined than ever. The Karamazovs, whose lives for several years have been made purgatory by Dominick, Caroline, and Nanny, especially Nanny, send in a modest bill for the schooling of the young people which Fortinbras has no intention of settling. It would seem unreasonable to pay for one's children to be taught to murder the English language and taught, apparently, nothing else whatever. Dominick, failing to get into Eton, has had to be sent to some dreadful school in Scotland. Besides, what did the Karamazovs do in the war? Nothing, according to Nanny, but flop in and out of a swimming pool. The Karamazovs come to England expecting to be thanked, feted, and paid, only to find that their friends have left for the Northern Capitals.

Now the Fortinbrases are getting on, over fifty. Dominick having come of age, they have broken the entail and sold everything, very badly, as the house is full of dry rot and the farms are let to tenants who cannot be dislodged. However, a little money does result from the sale. They arrange a mews flat behind Harrods where, generals once again, they will continue to cook and wash up for the rest of their days. They both still sit on endless committees, Fortinbras goes to the House of Lords, they kill themselves with overwork, and have never, except for their Army pay, earned one single penny. 'Aren't the Fortinbrases wonderful?' Well yes, in a way they are.

Now, while the Fortinbrases have the typical aristocratic outlook on money, the state of their finances is by no means typical. Most people, nowadays, take it for granted that the aristocracy is utterly impoverished, a view carefully fostered by the lords themselves. It takes a shooting affray, letting police and reporters into a country house, to remind the ordinary citizen that establishments exist where several men-servants wait on one young woman at dinner. There are still many enormous fortunes in the English aristocracy, into which income tax and death duties have made no appreciable inroads. Arundel, Petworth, Hatfield, Woburn, Hardwicke, Blenheim, Haddon, Drumlanrig, Alnwick, Stratfield Saye, Harewood, Knole, Knowsley, Wilton, Holkham, Glamis, Cullen, Cliveden, Highclere, Althorp, Mentmore—all vast houses—are still inhabited by lords who have inherited them, or by members of their families. This little list is a mere fraction of the whole. The treasures such houses contain are stupendous. When the Duke of Buccleuch came to visit the Louvre, the curator, who had been to England and seen the Duke's collection of French furniture, greeted him with the words: 'I apologize for the furniture of the Louvre, M. le Duc.'

Another English duke owns a collection of incunables second only to that formerly in the possession of the Kings of Spain, and more Grolier bindings than the Bibliothèque Nationale. A jeweller told me that out of the one hundred finest diamonds in the world, sixty are in English families. One could go on citing such instances indefinitely.

The English, so censorious of those foreigners (the French peasantry for instance) who do not pay their taxes as they should, have themselves brought tax evasion within legal limits to a fine art. Death duties can be avoided altogether if the owner of an estate gives it to his heir and then lives another five years. One agreeable result of this rule is that old lords are cherished as never before. Their heirs, so far from longing to step into their shoes, will do anything to keep them alive. Doctors and blood donors hover near them, they are not allowed to make the smallest effort, or to be worried or upset, and are encouraged to live in soft climates and salubrious spots.

The crippling effects of supertax also can be overcome in various ways by those who own large capital sums. The aristocrat can augment his fortune in many a curious manner, since he is impervious to a sense of shame (all aristocrats are: shame is a bourgeois notion). The lowest peasant of the Danube would stick at letting strangers into his house for 2s. 6d., but our dukes, marquesses, earls, viscounts, and barons not only do this almost incredible thing, they glory in it, they throw themselves into the sad commerce with rapture, and compete as to who among them can draw the greatest crowds. It is the first topic of conversation in noble circles today, the tourists being referred to in terms of sport rather than of cash—a sweep-stake on the day's run, or the bag counted after the shoot.

'I get twice as many as Reggie, but Bert does better than me.'

The baiting of the trap is lovingly considered.

'Mummy dresses up in her Coronation robes, they can't resist it.'

'I say, old boy, look out—you don't want to pay enter-tainment tax.'

'No, no—I've taken counsel's opinion.'

'We've started a pets' cemetery—a quid for a grave, three quid for a stone, and a fiver if Daphne writes a poem for it.'

Of course the fellow countrymen of people who will descend to such methods of raising cash imagine that they must be driven to it by direst need. The fact is they thoroughly enjoy it. Also it has become a matter of pol-icy to appear very poor. The lords are retrenching visi-bly, and are especially careful to avoid any form of osten-tation: for instance, only five of them saw fit to attend the last coronation in their family coaches. Coronets on lug-gage, motor-cars, and so on are much less used than for-merly. Aristocrats no longer keep up any state in

London, where family houses hardly exist now. Here many of them have shown a sad lack of civic responsibility, as we can see by looking at poor London today. At the beginning of this century practically all the residential part of the West End belonged to noblemen and the Crown. A more charming, elegant capital city would have been far to seek. To the Crown—more specifically, I believe, to King George V in person—and to two Dukes, Westminster and Bedford, we owe the fact that London is not yet exactly like Moscow, a conglomeration of dwellings. Other owners cheerfully sold their houses and 'developed' their property without a thought for the visible result. Park Lane, most of Mayfair, the Adelphi, and so on bear witness to a barbarity which I, for one, cannot forgive.

The lords have never cared very much for London, and are, in this respect, the exact opposite of their French counterparts who loathe the country. But even where his country house is concerned, the English nobleman, whose forbears were such lovers of beauty, seems to have lost all æsthetic sense, and it is sad to see the havoc he often brings to his abode, both inside and out. His ancestors spent months abroad, buying pictures and statues, which he cheerfully sells in order to spend months abroad. Should one of his guests perceive that a blackened square of canvas in a spare bedroom is a genuine Caravaggio, that picture will appear at Christies before you can say Jack Robinson, though there is no necessity whatever for such a sale. The Caravaggio buyer planted his estate with

avenues and copices and clumps of cedar trees. The
Caravaggio seller fiddles about with herbaceous borders,
one of the most hideous conceptions known to man. He
never seems to plant anything larger than a flowering
prunus, never builds ornamental bridges, or digs lakes, or
adds wings to his house. The last nobleman to build a
folly on his estate must have been Lord Berners and he
was regarded as foolish indeed to do such a thing. The
noble eccentric, alas, seems to be dying out. Lord Berners
was one, another was the late Duke of Bedford, pacifist,
zoologist, and a good man. One of the chapters of his
autobiography, I seem to remember, was headed 'Spiders
I have known', and he tells of one spider he knew whose
favourite food was roast beef and Yorkshire pudding. The
great days of patronage, too, are over, though there are
country houses which still shelter some mild literary
figure as librarian. The modern nobleman cannot, however, be blamed for no longer patronizing art, music, and
letters. Artists, musicians, and writers are today among
the very richest members of the community and even an
English aristocrat could hardly afford to maintain Mr.
Somerset Maugham, M. Stravinsky, or M. Picasso as part
of his establishment.

Voltaire very truly said that those who own are those
who wish to own: this wish seems to have left the English
lords. Divest, divest, is the order of the day. The nobleman used to study a map of his estate to see how it could
be enlarged, filling out a corner here, extending a horizon
there. Nowadays he has no such ambitions; he would
much rather sell than buy. The family is not considered as

Ancestors are no longer revered

some of the most ringing rows of all time

it used to be; the ancestors are no longer revered, indeed they are wilfully forgotten, partly perhaps from a feeling of guilt when all that they so carefully amassed is being so carelessly scattered. The dead are hardly mourned. 'Far the best for him', the children say, cheerfully (so long, of course, as he has lived the requisite five years). Nobody wears black any more. The younger generation is no longer planned for, and there is a general feeling of *'après nous le déluge'*.

The instinct of the lords to divest themselves of age-long influence and rights extends to their influence and rights in the Church. Most of them are members of the Church of England; though there are forty-seven Roman Catholics with seats in the House of Lords. On the whole, the lords, in common with most of their fellow country-men, have always regarded religious observance as a sort of patriotic duty. The Church is the Church of England and must be supported to show that we are not as for-eigners are. A friend of mine voiced this attitude during the war: 'Well, you know, I don't do fire-watching or Home Guard and I feel one must do something to help the war, so I always go to Church on Sunday.' I am sure he did not imagine that his prayers would drive back the German hordes; he went as a gesture of social solidarity. Hitherto, the livings of our Church have been the gift of landowners, who have generally chosen downright, mus-cular Christians of low Church leanings. 'Don't want lace and smells in my Church.' Zeal has always been frowned upon. As it is impossible to remove a parson once he is installed in his living, some of the most ringing rows of all time have been between the Manor and the Vicarage. Now, however, faithful to the spirit of divest, divest, the temporal lords are busily putting their livings at the disposal of their spiritual colleagues, the Bishops. Many people think that this will lead to more lace, more smells, and more un-English zeal in the Church, and indeed greatly alter its character. Incidentally, the marriage customs of the peerage have lately become very lax. One peer in eight has divested himself of his wife, and foreigners notice that there are rather more duchesses than dukes in London society today.

As for the House of Lords which gives the English aristocrat his unique position, Lord Hailsham, himself an unwilling member, says that the majority of peers are voting for its abolition 'with their feet', by simply neglecting their hereditary duties. It must be said that the number of regular attendants has never been very large, and the august chamber has always been characterized by an atmosphere of the dormitory if not of the morgue. This is distressing to an active young fellow like Lord Hailsham but it is nothing new. One of the merits of the Upper House has been to consist of a hard core of politicians reinforced now and then by experts, and only flooded out in times of crisis by all its members. These have hitherto proved not unrepresentative of public opinion. Now, however, it seems that it is hardly possible to get through the work, so small is the attendance.

Does this apparent abdication of the lords in so many different directions mean that the English aristocracy is in full decadence and will soon exist only like the appendix in the human body, a useless and sometimes harmful relic of the past? It would not be safe to assume so. The English lord has been nurtured on the land and is conversant with the cunning ways of the animal kingdom. He has often seen the grouse settle into the heather to rise and be shot at no more. He has noticed that enormous riches are not well looked on in the modern world and that in most countries his genus is extinct. It may be that he who for a thousand years has weathered so many a storm, religious, dynastic, and political, is taking cover in order to weather yet one more. It may be that he will succeed. He must, of course, be careful not to overdo the protective colouring. An aristocracy cannot exist as a secret society. Nor must he overdo an appearance of destitution. There is the sad precedent of George Neville who was deprived of his dukedom (Bedford) by act of Parliament because 'as is openly known he hath not, nor by inheritance may have, any livelihood to support the name, estate and dignity . . .'

But the English lord is a wily old bird who seldom overdoes anything. It is his enormous strength.

AN OPEN LETTER TO THE
HON^{BLE} MRS. PETER RODD
(NANCY MITFORD) ON
A VERY SERIOUS SUBJECT
FROM EVELYN WAUGH

AN OPEN LETTER TO THE HON^BLE MRS. PETER RODD (NANCY MITFORD) ON A VERY SERIOUS SUBJECT

DEAREST NANCY,

Were you surprised that your article on the English aristocracy caused such a to-do? I wasn't. I have long revered you as an agitator—agitatrix, *agitateuse?*—of genius. You have only to publish a few cool reflections on 18th-century furniture to set gangs on the prowl through the Faubourg St. Germain splashing the walls with 'Nancy, go home'. In England class distinctions have always roused higher feelings than national honour; they have always been the subject of feverish but very private debate. So, when you brought them into the open, of course everyone talked, of course the columnists quoted you and corrected you. Letters poured in to the various editors, many of them, I am told, unprintably violent. You were the subject of a literary competition (which produced very sad entries) and now here am I, late but implacable, chipping in too.

Should delicacy have restrained you? your friends anx-
iously ask. There are subjects too intimate for print.
Surely class is one? The vast and elaborate structure grew
up almost in secret. Now it shows alarming signs of dilap-
idation. Is this the moment to throw it open to the heavy-
footed public? Yes, I think it is, and particularly, as you
have done, to the literary public. My reproach is that, in
doing so, you have in your skittish way bamboozled a
great number of needy young persons. Have you ever
heard of the 'Butler Education Act'? I suppose not,
although it happened in the days when you still lived
among us. It was one of the things that politicians did
when no one was looking, towards the end of the war. It
has nothing at all to do with training male indoor-ser-
vants nor with instructing the designer of the 'Unknown
Political Prisoner' in the intricacies of his craft. The name
derives from the Mr. Butler who at the time of writing has
just knocked a few shillings off the price of my trousers.
Clearly he is a generous fellow. In his Education Act he
provided for the free distribution of university degrees to
the deserving poor. Very handy for splitting atoms and
that kind of thing, you will say. But many of Mr. Butler's
protégés choose, or are directed into, 'Literature'. I could
make your flesh creep by telling you about the new wave
of philistinism with which we are threatened by these sour
young people who are coming off the assembly lines in
their hundreds every year and finding employment as
critics, even as poets and novelists. L'École de Butler are
the primal men and women of the classless society. Their
novelists seem to be aware of the existence of a rather

more expensive world than their own—bars in which spirits are regularly drunk in preference to beer, loose women who take taxis, crooks in silk shirts—but of the ramifications of the social order which have obsessed some of the acutest minds of the last 150 years, they know less than of the castes of India. What can their critics hope to make of the undertones and innuendoes, the evocative, reminiscent epithets of say, Tony Powell or Leslie Hartley?

It was a worthy project to take them through a rudimentary course of social map-reading and no one should have been better qualified for the task than you with your host of friends in every class.

Nor was L'École de Butler your only source of pupils. Consider the cinema trade, the immigrant producers from God knows where who perhaps have never set foot in a private house in the kingdom. Their solecisms glare at us in blazing colour and shriek at us from amplifiers. At the BBC, a hive of addicts to the deplorable 'Dear Nancy Mitford' form of address, a huge mission field was white for your sickle. Eager, appealing eyes were turned to you through the cigarette smoke. Was it kind, dear Nancy, to pull their legs?

II

You very properly steer clear of the royal family and start your exposition with the peerage. You remark, correctly, that a title in England has a precise legal significance, as it has scarcely anywhere else, and that, partly from our system of primogeniture, titled people do not constitute a separate caste. But you go on to say that a man 'becomes an aristocrat as soon as he receives a title', ' . . . his outlook from now on will be the outlook of an aristocrat'. You know jolly well that that isn't true.

The relationship between aristocracy and nobility in England is certainly baffling. I do not suppose you could find any two people in complete agreement about it. My own estimate would be that about half the nobility are aristocrats and about two-thirds of the aristocracy are noble (in which catalogue I loosely include baronets and people descended in the male line from peers, whether or no they are themselves titled). There is no greater degree of social uniformity in the Upper House of Parliament than in the Commons. The official order of precedence is, of course, quite irrelevant in determining true social position. Ancestry, possessions, achievements, even humour and good looks, have their part in deciding real precedence.

You say: 'Ancestry has never counted much in England.' As a guide to human character, pedigrees are, I suppose, about as valuable as horoscopes. Some of the world's greatest men have resorted to astrologers and millions of subtle Asiatics direct their lives by them today. Learned opinion may change. It may be decided that there was something in the stars after all. My own scepticism about theories of inherited characteristics is based on the impossibility of identifying the real fathers in the ages when adultery was very common and divorce very rare. Whenever there is a scandal elderly persons will remark,

'Ah, that is the Fortinbras blood coming out', and explain that all their mothers' generation were irregularly conceived. But undoubtedly most of our fellow-countrymen attach great importance to ancestry. Take a look at the shelves marked 'Genealogy' in any large secondhand bookshop. You will find displayed at modest prices hundreds of volumes expensively produced, mostly during the last hundred years, for the sole purpose of exalting their authors' families. Genealogy is still as thriving a trade as it was in the days of Elizabeth I, when the Officers of Arms began fabricating the great pedigrees that link the despoilers of the Church with the age of chivalry. People in the last century have been caught filling their parish churches with bogus tombs. Scholars such as Round and Barron spent their lives in exposing fraudulent pedigrees and many who are not scholars, but who, like myself, cherish the delusion that we possess a 'historical sense', have felt the fascination of this sonorous and decorative pursuit.

However, you give us some genealogical figures. Are you sure you have got them right? I know you went to high authority for them, but I can't help wondering how much the present Officers of Arms regard themselves as bound in honour to support the decisions of their less scrupulous predecessors. You say that 382 peers have arms granted before 1485 *and have inherited them in the male line*. My italics, as they say; for the statement staggers me. Neither of us is an expert. We can only look about us and go by rough personal impressions. It seems to me that a remarkably large number of our ancient fam-

ilies have the entry 'assumed by royal licence the name
and arms' somewhere in their pedigrees. Look at the
Fortinbrases. Sly Ned Fartingbrass who got the estate at
the Dissolution was known to all. It was for his grandson
that the Heralds invented a link with the extinct cru-
saders, Fortinbras. The peerage was granted by Charles I
and failed in the male line in 1722 when Mr. Binks married the heiress and sat in the Commons as Mr.
Fortinbras-Binks, exercising the full political influence of
his wife's family. His son, who called himself Mr. Binks-
Fortinbras, married well, could return two members; he
was rewarded by a peerage; Fortinbras, in the second cre-
ation. From that time Binks was dropped and the stolen
coat of Fortinbras moved across, with the connivance of
the College of Heralds, to the first quarter.

You say that 65 existing baronies were created before
1711. Do you include the quaint house of Strabolgi?

Noble families die out almost as fast as new ones are
created. I have just taken a sample from Burke's *Peerage
and Baronetage* 1949 and compared it with the issue for
1885. The volumes fall open, need I say it? at Redesdale.
Of the succeeding dozen names only one (and that, incidentally, a family of foreign origin) is to be found in the
earlier edition; and of the twelve families who followed
Redesdale in 1885, six are already extinct. That is a big
turnover in two generations. Perhaps you will argue that
it is the new families who die out, since the older the family, the further you can cast back for an heir. Well, looking round, the feudal overlords in the district where I live
were the Berkeleys. That earldom has lately become

extinct. And their next-door neighbours, who bear a medieval name and arms, have borne and changed no less than five surnames in the last eight generations as the property devolved on female heirs. I think you should have questioned your pursuivant more closely before accepting his figures.

III

The Fortinbrases are a delicious vignette, typical of your fictions. I find one fault only. Surely they should have more children? Impotence and sodomy are socially O.K. but birth control is flagrantly middle-class. But you invented them, I know, to illustrate your theme that aristocrats can't or won't make money. I could remind you of half a dozen prosperous and industrious City men of impeccable origins but I should have to admit that they have not worn well. The acceptance of high living and leisure as part of the natural order is a prerequisite of the aristocratic qualities and achievements. The debonair duke living by his wits, so popular on the stage, soon grows to resemble the plebeian crook. His brother who goes into business and sticks to it and makes good, is soon indistinguishable from his neighbours in Sunningdale. You should have said, not that aristocrats can't make money in commerce, but that when they do, they become middle-class.

It is here that we reach the topic that has caused the pother —the supposed gulf between what you inelegantly describe as 'U and non-U'.

This gulf exists in every English mind. What has

Birth control is flagrantly middle-class

shocked your critics is that you fix it where you do, definitely, arbitrarily, and, some would say, capriciously. There is an unwholesome contemporary appetite— the product, perhaps, of psychiatry and the civil service —for categories of all kinds. People seem to be comforted instead of outraged when they are told that their eccentricities entitle them to membership in a class of 'psychological types'. They are inured to filling in forms which require a 'description' of themselves and their houses. So they have fastened with avidity on the section of your comprehensive essay which pretends to provide the mechanism for grading themselves and their friends.

Everything turns on 'the grand old name of gentleman'. We have no equivalent phrase in English to *'noblesse oblige'*. All precepts of manners and morals define the proper conduct of 'gentlemen'. Lord Curzon, a paragon of aristocratic usage, when, as Chancellor of the University, he was shown the menu of a proposed entertainment of the King at Balliol, remarked succinctly: 'No gentleman has soup at luncheon'; he did not say: 'No monarch . . .' or 'No marquis . . .' He appealed above the standards of court or castle to the most elusive standard in the world.

When I was last in Palestine I asked a Zionist how he defined a Jew. Immigrants from every climate from China to Peru were jostling round us. There were atheist Slavs, orthodox semites from the ghettoes of Morocco and negroes from the Upper Nile who are reputed to eat snakes. It seemed a pertinent question. He answered: 'Everyone who thinks he is a Jew, is one.'

In the same way, the basic principle of English social life is that *everyone* (everyone, that is to say, who comes to the front door) *thinks he is a gentleman.* There is a second principle of almost equal importance: *everyone draws the line of demarcation immediately below his own heels.* The professions rule out the trades; the Services, the professions; the Household Brigade, the line regiments; squires, squireens; landed families who had London houses ruled out those who spent all the year at home; and so on, in an infinite number of degrees and in secret, the line is, or was, drawn. It is essentially a process of ruling *out*. If you examine the accumulated code of precepts which define 'the gentleman' you will find that almost all are negative.

Few well-bred people are aware, still less observant, of more than a small fraction of this code. Most people have a handful of taboos, acquired quite at random. Usually at an impressionable age someone has delivered a judgement which has taken root. The lack of reason in these dooms makes them the more memorable, and no subsequent experience mitigates their authority.

For example, there is a cousin of yours, a jolly, badly dressed baron. He and I were talking one day when there passed an acquaintance, a grandee, a member of the Jockey Club, your cousin's superior and *a fortiori* mine. Your cousin, not a very serious man normally, regarded this sleek, russet figure with aversion and said, with deep seriousness: 'My father told me that no gentleman ever wore a brown suit.'

Another cousin of yours, of more august descent, is a

man notorious for the grossness of his vocabulary. He has only to hear a piece of *argot* from the Bowery to adopt it as his own. But once, in early youth, he was sharply corrected for calling a kinsman his 'relative' or 'relation'. He cannot remember which, but both words have become anathema. Of all the sage advice poured out on him by schoolmasters and clergymen and dons and commanding officers, that alone remains, and if either word is used in his hearing, he starts as though stung and, being what he is, he rounds on the speaker with abuse.

All nannies and many governesses, when pouring out tea, put the milk in first. (It is said by tea fanciers to produce a richer mixture.) Sharp children notice that this is not normally done in the drawing-room. To some this revelation becomes symbolic. We have a friend you may remember, far from conventional in other ways, who makes it her touchstone. 'Rather MIF, darling', she says in condemnation.

There is the question of ichthyotomy. Some years ago a friend of mine, in a novel, described the wife of a Master of Hounds as using a fish-knife. I warned him that this would cause offence and, sure enough, the wife of a neighbouring MFH got as far as this passage and threw the book from her crying: 'The fellow can't even write like a gentleman', while all the time, higher in the social scale, at some (I am told at many) of the really august stately homes fish-knives have been in continuous use for nearly a hundred years.

They were a Victorian invention in pretty general use in polite society in the 60s. Certain old-fashioned people, of the kind who today eschew the telephone, derided the gadgets, which soon began to appear among the wedding presents of professional persons. The old-fashioned people scratched away with two forks and also picked their teeth at table, which was considered low by smart Londoners. The old-fashioned people won through an odd alliance with the aesthetes. When people began moving their Chippendale chairs down from the attics, they began denuding their tables of Victorian silver. In our life-time we have seen few fish-knives in private houses and many toothpicks. But it has all been a matter of fashion not of class.

I could multiply examples almost without end. There is practically no human activity or form of expression which at one time or another in one place or another, I have not heard confidently condemned as plebeian, for generations of English have used the epithets 'common' and 'middle-class' as general pejoratives to describe anything which gets on their nerves.

It is natural to the literary mind to be unduly observant of the choice of words. Logan Pearsall Smith was the classical case. I met him once only. He did not speak to me until we stood on the doorstep leaving. He then said: 'Tell me, how would you describe the garment you are wearing? A greatcoat? An overcoat? A topcoat?' I replied: 'Overcoat.' 'Ah, would you? Yes. Most interesting. And, tell me, would that also be the usage of an armigerous admiral?'

That way lay madness and I fear that if you are taken too seriously you and Professor Ross may well drive your readers into the bin. When in your novel you made 'Uncle Matthew' utter his catalogue of irrational prohibitions, you were accurately recording a typical conversational extravagance. When you emerge *in propria persona* as the guide to Doric youth, you are more mischievous. Of course, it is broadly true that twenty-five or thirty years ago the phrases you dub 'U', came more naturally to most ladies and gentlemen than those you condemn. Traces of that lingo survive today here and there among well-brought-up young people. But fashionable usage was even then in constant transition. Every family and every set always had its private vocabulary and syntax and still has. I know people whose terms of condemnation are quite simply NLU and NLO ('not like us' and 'not like one'). Everyone has always regarded any usage but his own as either barbarous or pedantic. Phrases that were originally adopted facetiously, in inverted commas as it were, pass into habitual use; the chic jargon of one decade—Philip Sassoon's 'I couldn't like it more', for instance—becomes the vulgarism of the next; words once abhorred, like 'week-end', become polite. Consider the influence of the USA. There are few families without American connexions today and American polite vocabulary is very different from ours. We fight shy of abbreviations and euphemisms. They rejoice in them. The blind and maimed are called 'handicapped', the destitute, 'underprivileged'. 'Toilet' is pure American (but remember that our 'lavatory' is equally a euphemnism). Remember too that the American vocabulary is pulverized between two stones, refinement and overstatement. *'O let me not be mentally ill,*

not mentally ill, sweet heaven' sounds odd, but in the USA
'mad' merely means 'cross'. If Professor Ross's Finns or
your literary disciples wander out into the English world
armed with your lexicon, seeking to identify the classes
they encounter, they will drop many bricks. For habits of
speech are not a matter of class but of society and on the
whole English people do not congregate exclusively or by
preference with their social equals.

Look back twenty-five years to the time when there
was still a fairly firm aristocratic structure and the country was still divided into spheres of influence among
hereditary magnates. My memory is that the grandees
avoided one another unless they were closely related.
They met on state occasions and on the race-course.
They did not frequent one another's houses. You might
find almost anyone in a ducal castle—convalescent,
penurious cousins, advisory experts, sycophants, gigolos
and plain blackmailers. The one thing you could be sure
of not finding was a concourse of other dukes. English
society, it seemed to me, was a complex of tribes, each
with its chief and elders and witch-doctors and braves,
each with its own dialect and deity, each strongly xeno-
phobic.

Dons by habit mark everything α, β or γ. They speak of
'upper, middle and lower classes'. Socialists speak of 'cap-
italists, bourgeois, intellectuals, workers'. But these sim-
ple categories do not apply in England. Here there is very
little horizontal stratification apart from the single, vari-
able, great divide specified above. There is instead precedence, a single wholly imaginary line (a Platonic idea)

extending from Windsor to Wormwood Scrubs, of separate individuals each justly and precisely graded. In the matter of talking together, eating together, sleeping together, this mysterious line makes little difference, but every Englishman is sharply aware of its existence, and this awareness often spices these associations very pleasantly.

IV

It is when we come to the last part of your article, much the most important part, which has nevertheless attracted least notice, that my amusement at your prank becomes a little strained.

'The English lord is a wily old bird' you take as your text, and your theme is that he is enormously rich. He pays neither taxes nor death duties. He 'glories' in turning his house into a public museum. He has given up London simply because he is not witty enough to keep a salon. He sells his pictures because he does not appreciate them. He prefers herbaceous borders and flowering shrubs to the formal parterres which require two dozen gardeners. His reduced circumstances are all a hoax. He is biding his time until the present craze for equality has passed, when he will re-emerge in all his finery to claim all his privileges, to ravish village brides and transport poachers to Botany Bay.

Can you really believe any of this, even living, as you do, so remote from the scene you describe? Not long ago an American cutie, married to a Labour politician, published a book propounding the same argument. Everyone

tolerantly asked: 'What can an American cutie married to
a Labour politician hope to know of such things? Ask her
to dinner and let her see for herself.' But what are we to say
now when Nancy, Queen of the Hons, comes out with the
same malicious errors? The English, you should remember, have a way of making jokes about their disasters, but
you would find, if you lived here, that the loudest jokes
about opening Stately Homes are made by the wives who
have recent and perhaps direful associations with them,
rather than by the husbands. Half Bowood, you should
know, is being demolished because its owner prefers priv-
acy. I am not familiar with the household accounts of the
few magnates who still preserve a recognizable ghost of
their former establishments, but I am pretty sure something has to be sold every year to keep going. But instead
of expostulating with you let me turn to your dupes and
tell them two facts which you have never attempted to
hide, bless you, but which are not well known.

The first is rather endearing. You were at the vital age
of twelve when your father succeeded to his peerage, and
until less than a year before there was little likelihood of
his ever succeeding. It was a great day for 'Hons' when
you and your merry sisters acquired that prefix of nobility. Hitherto it had been the most shadowy of titles, never
spoken, and rarely written. You brought it to light,
emphasized and aspirated, and made a glory of it. And
with that magic vocable came (very briefly it is true) a
sensational change of fortune. If your uncle had not been
killed in action, if your posthumous cousin had been a boy,
all you enchanting children would have been whisked

You regard Lloyd George as a great man

away to a ranch in Canada or a sheep-run in New Zealand. It is fascinating to speculate what your careers would then have been. Anyway, at that impressionable age an indelible impression was made; Hons were unique and lords were rich.

The other fact is not nice. You are a socialist, as devoted and as old fashioned as the American cutie. As you confess in your article, you regard Lloyd George as a great man (and, we must suppose, as a great aristocrat too in his last days). You are dedicated to the class-war. Has the whisper reached you from our bleak island, as you recline in elegant seclusion, that the cause of 'Social Justice' is now being pleaded by the Hons? Alertly studied, your novels reveal themselves as revolutionary tracts and here, in your essay, you speak out boldly: 'Hear me, comrades. I come from the heart of the enemy's camp. You think they have lost heart for the fight. I have sat with them round their camp fires and heard them laughing. They are laughing at *you*. They are not beaten yet, comrades. Up and at them again.'

Is that what you are really saying, Nancy? I hope you are just teasing, as I am. I hope. I wonder.

Fondest love,
EVELYN

POSH LINGO

By

'STRIX'

POSH LINGO

Miss NANCY MITFORD'S article on the English Aristocracy in *Encounter* has given rise to much pleasurable discussion. Most of this has centred on U-words. This 'useful formula' (as Miss Mitford rather charitably calls it; I am sure that she herself speaks but rarely of the H-bomb or the V-sign) was invented by Professor Alan Ross, of Birmingham University, and used by him in a paper on 'Upper Class English Usage', which was published last year in the bulletin of a learned society in Finland.

Before pushing on to the less etymological aspects of her theme Miss Mitford mentions, as a factor liable to confuse still further a situation already sufficiently illogical and obscure, the frequent use, by those who in fact know better, of non-U words as a joke; and I am sure that a sense of parody is a formative influence in the case of U-slang. Non-U speakers, when they deliberately use what they believe to be U-words, are apt to make some attempt at mimicry, and phrases like *'I say, that's jolly decent (frightfully sporting, absolutely topping) of you, old man'* are delivered in a sort of Western Brothers accent. U-speakers, playing the same gambit for the same purpose only the other way round, tend to rely for their comic effect on the incongruity, upon their lips, of the words themselves. *'Ta ever so'*, *'a nice lie-down'*, *'one for the road'* —the use of such expressions is a mild form of skittishness; but to deliver them in a non-U accent would be facetious, and anyhow it is funnier—in so far as it is funny at all—to pronounce them in patrician or at least sophisticated tones.

In this way bits of non-U slang earn temporary and rather short-lived promotion. *Wizard*, for instance, started in the war-time RAF, graduated to schoolboy usage after the war and achieved for a time lodgement in the parody department of U-slang. Much the same, I suspect, has happened to *smashing*. I believe this sort of process to be much commoner than it used to be. The classes mix more (especially, during National Service, at their most slang-prone age), grown-ups see more of their children, and all ranks of society are bombarded by the radio and films[1] with the same new catch-words. I don't believe, for instance, that in its day *stunning*, though of comparatively refined origins, could ever have achieved the social success of *smashing*.

Professor Ross notes, I am sure correctly, a decline in the use of slang, to which 'U-speakers (particularly young ones) were rather addicted . . . in the nineties and at least up to 1914'. The point about slang words is that they

---

[1] Both non-U words. The *wireless* and the *cinema* are the U-versions.

should be expendable, and I always suspect that, in the rare cases where slang becomes—so to speak—frozen into a totemistic institution, the effect is stultifying. Winchester, for instance, has an elaborate vocabulary, known as 'notions', which every new boy must master, which was last codified by Sir Stafford Cripps and which has not in any important respect altered for the last four centuries; and it seems possible that, in so far as the word 'Wykehamist' can be said to comprise any uncongenial undertones, they may partly have their origins in the obligatory use of a specialized *lingua franca* at a formative age.

Eton, by contrast, not only uses very little slang but tends to use less and less. Perhaps one of the reasons for this is that, as U-families have grown smaller and the barriers between children and adults have largely disappeared, incomprehensible words—which once impressed younger brothers and sisters as a badge of maturity—have lost, if not their audience-appeal, most of their audience. It is certainly true that slang[1] has been on the decrease at Eton for the last fifty years. A reasonable deduction is that Etonians, more and more emancipated at home and at all times free to adapt the outward pattern of their school-society, subconsciously recognize in schoolboy slang a form of parochialism. Today the note of par-

---

[1] Here I mean slang in the sense of a tribal *patois* (e.g. *scug*, an inconsiderable or unworthy person; *float*, a mistake) as opposed to the adoption of modish catch-phrases (e.g. *keen*, ostentatiously efficient; *smooth*, flashy-urbane).

ody—a powerful influence (as I believe) in modern U-usage, and perhaps the deadliest weapon in the armoury of class-warfare—is creeping in at Eton. Twenty-five years ago a boy at Eton would have been as unlikely to call the Headmaster (then generally known as the Head Beak) the Head Man as he would have been to call 'Cave!', to exclaim 'What a jape!' or to employ any of the other expressions found in books like *Teddy Lester, Captain of Cricket*. Today the first of these usages is common.

Interest in the study of U-speech has been arbitrarily awakened. I think myself that this interest is unhealthy and contrary to the national interest. Very few of our institutions, and still fewer of our imponderable quirks and aberrations, are improved by being made self-conscious; and we should all, I am sure, be loth to see the whole thing sublimated into a kind of etymological folk-dance.

One of the reasons why this fate threatens it is to be found in Potterism. *Gamesmanship* and *Lifemanship* presented expedients, often involving the use of pseudo-U phraseology, for scoring off an 'opponent'. In fact it is a basic convention of U-speech never to do this.

Let me illustrate this point. Professor Ross is right when he says that a U-speaker, invited to stay at Shinwell Hall, Salop,[1] would say only *'I'm going to Shinwell'*.

---

[1] Miss Mitford, I believe, would write Shropshire for Salop. The thoughtful student may well prefer to follow the usage on his hostess's notepaper. If he is summoned at the last minute by reply-paid telegram he will be spared a hideous dilemma.

Now this usage confers upon Shinwell Hall the status of
what for lack of a more revolting phrase can be called a U-
institution. It presupposes that the person addressed
knows, at the least, the identity of the owners of Shinwell
Hall, and, since the number of guest-prone country
houses in the household-word category is no longer large,
'*I'm going to Shinwell*' is a statement which (as a non-U
speaker might put it) indubitably confers a social *cachet*.
These words would accordingly only be used in conversation with another U-speaker. A person who either

(a) would be unlikely to know what 'Shinwell' meant, or

(b) might think that the speaker was seeking to im-
press him by claiming the entrée to a household-word
house, would probably be told ' *I'm going to stay with some
people in Shropshire*'.

For it cannot be too strongly emphasized that U-speech
is not—as many believe—an arrogant and 'snooty' institution, used mainly, like lorgnettes, for outfacing non-U-
speakers. It is the natural idiom of a comparatively small
class and exists to further the purposes of communication
within that class. As in the instance given above, its usages
are avoided or paraphrased in conversation with a non-U-
speaker to whom they might seem obscure or ostentatious;
and in certain cases a U-word may be replaced by a non-U
word (e.g. a U-speaker giving orders to (say) a gardener or
a groom will say 'You'd better finish that job *after you've
had your dinner*' and not '*after lunch*[1]').

All classes share this tendency to adapt their own idiom

[1] Still less '*after luncheon*', a U-usage obligatory in writing but
barely permissible in speech.

when talking to members of other classes, their motives in doing so being generally a mixture of delicacy and expediency. To take an obvious example, a Cockney private soldier may refer to his wife as his 'trouble and strife' when talking to his friends in the sort of relaxed atmosphere which promotes the use of rhyming slang; but he will not dream of employing this usage when applying to his company commander for compassionate leave.

It is worse than useless to try and trace any sort of principle, rule, tradition or preference in the light of which the line is drawn between U-usage and non-U-usage. Why should *'the wife'* (for *'my wife'*) be non-U, *'the children'* common to both, and *'the dog'* (implying a sort of communal dog, for whom nobody in particular is responsible) very slightly non-U?

At times it seems as though U-speakers had a leaning towards understatement. *'A moderate effort'* is the U-equivalent of *'a damn bad show'*; when applied to an individual, *'boring'*, though it may sometimes mean merely what it says, is at present often used to express disapproval or even anger in contexts where non-U-speakers would employ a harsher and more explicit pejorative. At other times, however, U-speech shows a pronounced trend in the opposite direction, towards overstatement. *'I had the wind up'* is a non-U admission: a U-speaker would say *'I was petrified with fear'*. As in the eighteenth century, U-conversation is larded with vehement and extreme adjectives *(ghastly, frightful, disastrous, nauseating)*, but they are no more intended to be taken *au pied de la lettre* than the unprintable epithets so freely used by soldiers. Perhaps it is true to say that a relish for incongruity is one of the very few identifiable characteristics of an argot in which a dull party can be called *'a disaster'*, while a disaster (on the battlefield) can equally well be called *'a party'*.

Military U-speech (talking of battlefields) is a very highly specialized subject because of the innumerable differences in regimental usage. I believe, for instance, that *mufti* (for *plain clothes)* is not merely permissible but obligatory in some perfectly reputable regiments; there may even be units where officers are allowed to refer to their commanding officer as *'the C.O.'* (I am told that in the RAF the adjutant is often spoken of as *'the adj.'*). Before leaving this debatable and almost unexplored ground I must record my impression that, although it is perfectly U to be *wounded*, it is slightly U-er to be *hit*.

We have already glanced at the inconsistencies which bedevil the use of *the* (for *my*, *our*, *a*, etc.). Here are some more: *'The village are livid'* becomes, in non-U, *'Our village is up in arms'*. *'We're going to the theatre'*[1] becomes *'We're going to* (or, worse, *doing) a show'*. Occasionally one seems to stumble on a clue which may lead one out of this pointless labyrinth. A Yorkshire landowner may, when away from home, say in August *'THE grouse are no good this year'* and in November *'My pheasants are no good this year'*; the distinction (not only valid but decorous) drawn here is

---

[1] *'We're going to the play'* is obsolescent and its use, therefore, slightly affected.

I understand that in some quite reputable *regiments it is
not only permissible but* obligatory *to call plain clothes
MUFTI!!*

between 'the' grouse, whose abundance or otherwise is attributable to various minor Acts of God from which his neighbours have suffered or benefited more or less equally, and 'his' pheasants, whose welfare is (theoretically) directly affected by his strategy and his keepers'[1] tactics.

All tradition is bequeathed, however distrustfully, to the young. The U-young have not been dragooned about the use of words in the way their parents were; and they have ingested a richer, more variegated slice of the marzipan of English usage than reached, in the ordinary way of business, the gizzards of their elders. If they are sensible and civic, they will try and iron out these pregnant but elusive nuances and strive for a clear, classless medium of communication in which all say 'Pardon?' and none say 'What?', every ball is a dance and every man's wife is 'the' wife.

I shall be surprised, and disappointed, if they make the slightest endeavour to impoverish our extraordinary national life by doing anything of the sort.

[1] This usage *(keepers* in the plural) is rare but permissible in certain contexts; *'my head-keeper'* is non-U. If talking to friends who might reasonably be expected to know it, the man's name will be used, but should not be prefixed by *'old'*. In all other circumstances the U-usage is *'my keeper'* (cf. the U-mother's *'my Nannie').* I am not yet adequately informed about the vocabulary of U-lunatics.

WHAT U-FUTURE?

by

CHRISTOPHER SYKES

WHAT U-FUTURE?

ALL groups talk a particular language. That statement is not open to question and I think it is not a matter to be regretted either. It is the natural way of things. You say something one way which the lawyer says another way. If you used the lawyer's language you would sound (if you were myself) a pretentious fool parading learning that you were without, and the lawyer using your language might sound as though he were trying to be more 'human', more of a terribly decent ordinary chap about it all than it is likely he can be. The lawyer and you understand this and lose no respect for each other. Same with doctors, same with sailors, same with all other craftsmen. We recognize each other's groups and do not necessarily assume that our group is superior to other groups. But there is a point where professional language turns into professional jargon. Here usage is very much open to objection if it is ever used except within the group. It is reasonable to insist that all members of all professional groups must be intelligible to people outside. A doctor who can only talk like a text-book may leave you in serious doubt as to your state of health. A clergyman who can only address his congregation in the difficult terms which theologians use among themselves might not succeed in his professional duty of saving souls. Some art historians and literary critics would not appear to agree with this, to judge from their public play with professional slang, but the great and unforgotten experts and critics have understood the point and obeyed the rules it implies.

Out of the different languages of different professions, more than from other sources, the master language of a people is formed and enriched and kept alive. Shakespeare found a vast instrument at his command, not because he had been preceded by generations of etymologists but by people who had 'frothed and lived'. He owed things to trade language, legal language, theological language, naval language, military language, official language, and the language of fools, but pretty well nothing to anyone's jargon. (When he used jargon for joking purposes, the most frequent result for us is the patch of boredom.) Down with those who would refuse men the right to professional speech! Down yet further with those who think professions honoured by the public use of their private terms!

It is wrong, however, to conclude that all a language needs is a thriving national activity behind it, and the consequent enrichment of idiom. That would lead straight to disaster, to so enormous and unmanageable a vocabulary that the language would ultimately split into dialects. Builders are necessary, but so are demolition men. There must be 'reducing agents' in a language: people who keep the inward flow of words to manageable proportions, and who throw out useless old junk. In France they have an academy for the purpose, and here we have a stalwart band of etymologists who strive in a dedicated spirit to keep our language graceful, vigorous and practical. All power to their elbows, pens and tongues, but I believe that their good work for human speech counts for very little beside the powerful and wholly irrational movements of fashion. Newspaper fashion, pub fashion, cinema fashion, popular song fashion, these all tend to work within little vocabularies. But the great, the most desired fashion, has always been that of 'the best society', of 'the fashionable', of the people who astonish by mysterious arts of 'chic'. The vocabulary of these rare beings is never large and is rigidly adhered to.

This sort of fashion is kept going by snobbism, and snobbism has its defenders, notably those who see in it a love of the best possible, of a pursuit of perfection. These champions of a widely shared weakness might, however, add vigour to their argument by remembering that the snobs of the world, those who would lisp in the accents of the earthly paradise, do a recognizable service to language by keeping its structure down to a sensible size. There are such things as 'vogue words' as Logan Pearsall Smith liked to call them, many of which act as additions to vocabulary, but there are a far greater number of words discarded by vogue.

It is tempting to suppose that this constant dismissal of useful and inoffensive items of speech by the fashionable is part of the conservatism which is a natural characteristic of the well-to-do, but to suppose this is to miss the essential nature of fashion. Not only is it a continually changing thing, but a continually mad thing. Consider only the case of umbrellas. There was a time when the western users of umbrellas, men who had learned refinements of living in Asia, were so ill thought of that they were persecuted in the streets. That was conservatism. Then there came a time when umbrellas were recognized for what they were and became fashionable. That was rational progress. But the progress, because it involved fashion, could not proceed in a logical line. To this day it is thought a fitting thing for the fashionable U-man (to borrow Nancy Mitford's delightful borrowing) to wield an umbrella in the streets of London, but unspeakably un-U for the same man to wield it in country fields, unless he be a clergyman. Suppose that after lunch in a U-house a family of brothers go to the home farm for a visit of inspection on a rainy day. The Earl of Thing, and his brother Major the Hon. So-and-So Thingummy, must wear caps and mackintoshes, but the third brother, Canon the Hon. Such-and-Such Thingummy, can perfectly well take an umbrella with him, and his two brothers can perfectly well huddle to his side and shelter under his umbrella with him, but not under their own, though they possess numerous umbrellas between them. The Duke of Wellington is said to have used an umbrella on the field of battle, but despite his example (and he was very much a U-man), the British Army (unlike any other western army) has never been issued with this necessary equipment. In umbrellas, indeed, we find a perfect illustration

Unspeakably un-U . . . unless he be a clergyman

of the unpredictability of U-behaviour, neither conserva-
tive nor progressive, following example at the top or following mob-prejudice with equal determination. This
unpredictability makes U-speech so perplexing that no
rules can account for its pattern.

My generation was in its infancy when the cinema came
into being; I mean as a big permanent thing in our lives.
My parents, in my first days, did not quite know what
word to use for it. The real right people called it 'Kīnēma';
the rabble called it 'the pictures'; the ordinary people in the
middle called it 'the cinematograph', or 'cinema' for short.
If U-speakers had been real conservatives they would have
supported the potentates like Lord Curzon who said
'Kīnēma' to the end of his days. They would have disci-
plined their women into the same observance, would have
forced it on the crowd. As it is, they acquiesced in the semi-
learned 'cinema' which has the advantage of sounding
English and fitting neatly into our speech. (It could easily
be the name of a vegetable. Now then, dear, eat up your
sprouts and cinema, and make us all proud of you.)

Possibly because the cinema did not have a U-origin, it
could not, without affectation, have a U-name. But it is
interesting to note that the plebeian term 'Talkie', once
generally accepted, has been dethroned in its turn in
favour of its victim. This is a triumph of middle-class reason. Dukes and the lowest of commoners all say 'cinema'
now.

Then again, when I was a child my father, who looked
upon himself, I think, as a man of U-speech, would talk of
'going to town' meaning 'going to London'. The phrase

had a pleasant ring of ancient snobbism, being an English adaptation of the Greek and Roman fashion of referring to the Capital as 'The City': 'ἡ πόλὶς'; 'Urbs'; Roma Magna Mater! There was an aristocratic origin if ever there was one, but by the time my generation was grown up we looked on 'going to Town' as the worst of solecisms and used to mouth the phrase to each other amid howls of merriment. It was thought to be typical of a country bumpkin's effort to be smart. So, like the grandeur that was Rome, and the glory that was Greece, 'town' for London vanished with 'Kīnēma'.

But at least reasons of a sort can be adduced for such additions and rejections of words as those cited above. In many more cases, as with U-usage of umbrellas, no reasons can be imagined at all, except those of passion or delusion. The latter is a potent influence. Upper classes being of their very nature withdrawn and self-confident often suppose that their personal pleasures are supported by the considered approval of mankind. A notable Derbyshire magnate has been heard exhorting men to abominate the frequently used term 'car'. 'Nobody,' he has been reported to roar, 'nobody, except the foulest *canaille*, ever speaks or ever has spoken of a "car"—a cāāāh, forsooth—still less of a "motor"—ugh!—or of an "aut-oe-moe-bēēl"! Motor-car is what they say! Motor-car! Motor-car! MOTOR-CAR!' In the same way there are secluded lords who maintain that in gentle usage the word 'wood' has no meaning in the English language except in connection with port, bowls, and fire, and a Gloucestershire landowner believes that persons of family always refer to the wines of Bordeaux as 'clart' to rhyme with 'cart'. The latter delusion shows an impulse towards gentility, 'clart' having a decidedly dandyish sound, but impulses away from gentility are just as common. I used to know an elderly husband and wife, both of whom were of ducal descent, who talked with strong cockney accents, and the vogue for vulgarity of expression and pronunciation in a later generation, among highly placed persons in the 'twenties, was one of the most notorious oddities of that outlandish period.

The charm and interest of fashion lies in the way it reflects, either by stress or reaction, the mood of any time. At the present moment fashion is inclined to react: the fashionable man or woman tends to lead a life as un-typical as possible, but this has not often been so in the past and is unlikely to be so for ever in the future. I can perhaps illustrate my meaning here by working myself up into a prophetic state of mind, fancying myself through the mists as holding in my hands Number 1224 of 'Encounter' of September 2055, and reading therein an article on the subject of manners and customs among the upper or top-classes as they are likely to be called, written by a lady in a position to know the truth about this matter. Her words swim into legibility and 'Whenever I am asked', she seems to have, or to be going to have written, 'Whenever I am asked to write something about T-manners and T-customs etc. I say No, as I am always accused of being a snob whenever I do. But then they told me that there was so much interest in Topivity that really I ought to write about T-life from the T-point of view and from

T-experience, as otherwise people will go on getting all their ideas about the Top class from the absurd pictures of them which we find in the theatre, or the 6-D cinema or the Telepathic Screen. This rather "got me", as my great-great-aunt Nancy Mitford would have said, so I said, yes, oke.

'T-ness changes a lot and there are no definite rules about how to be T. I am just old enough to remember when it was ultra-T to go exploring on the moon, and when the Mare Imbrium used to be called "The snob's paradise". Nowadays the Moon is the very acme of Middle Classiness and to be described as "lunar" is rather what to be called "suburban" used to be to people in the time of my great-great-aunt. I suppose the reason is that once the moon was air-conditioned and colonized lots of T-people who'd got in a jam went there and it became a centre of sham T-society, and if there is anything that makes for untopivity it is anything sham-T. Anyway no T-person would ever dream of going there now unless he bloody well had to.

'Then although T-people know in a tick whether the other is T or not from the way they talk, it is difficult to say just why. Our ancestors were just as T-conscious as us but their speechways were as different as you can imagine. For instance, in an etiquette book of the last century, published in 1964 for the guidance of Office of Works officials at the Shakespeare fourth centenary celebrations, I find this: "In good society it is essential not to drop the aitch." This may have been true in my great-great-aunt's, or even in my grandmother's time, but can greater nonsense be

imagined today? Again I find in a quite modern grammar
the amazing assertion that care should be devoted to the
pronunciation of "th" as a lisping "S" and to suppressing
the terminal "g" in "ng" endings. This again is just miserable Middle Class aping of what they learn at second
hand. If any peer, I mean any real T-peer, were to say
"nothing" according to these rules, instead of the usual
"nuffink", he would either be thought to be joking, or, if it
wasn't known who he was (which is more or less impossible) would be suspected of imposture. T-people have
never since the 18th century gone in for linguistic exacti-
tude, and the idea that they still do is chiefly the fault of
the ridiculous pictures of aristocratic life which are the
mainstay of our popular theatre. People are often aston-
ished when I tell them that all duchesses say "tit fer"
rather than "hat", and that no duke would dream of referring to his children except as his "God forbids". It is a
long time since I heard a peer mention his wife in terms
other than "trouble and strife".

'The same sort of thing is true of clothes. Women's
clothes can't be docketed into T and non-T because fash-
ions change so much that all you can say is that it's un-T
to be in advance of fashion, or just a bit behind it, but very
T to be in fashion or right out of it. At the moment it is,
as it always has been, un-T for women to wear shorts at a
ball, but it may not stay like that for ever. You can't tell.
But men's clothes change so little that they have become
full of T-pointers. No T-peer (I simply haven't got time
for baronets) would ever appear anywhere with his
trousers tied up with string or in shoes that were not a

pair, or without socks in London even in summer. (Hot weather T-usage is very strange, by the way. It is perfectly oke for a T-man, or a "gent" as they used to be called, to put his handkerchief on his head with a knot at each corner, but to wear a newspaper as protection against the sun is thought utterly frightful.) The 6-D cinema idea that when dining out changed a peer always wears a tie with his suit is of course just silly romanticism, like the persistent belief that he never misses his weekly shave and bath, but it is, however, true that a T-man never dines out without putting on a collar if he's wearing a suit, but he does not wear a suit every time he dines out! That again is a stage idea—part of the theatrical mania to make T-people out as more glamorous and much more old-fashioned than they are. A T-dinner party is usually depicted in the more popular cinema and Telly as an assembly where everyone sits round a table, the men in suits and the women in skirts, eating various "courses" of food, and doing nothing but eat and talk and sip wine! No one says "Cor" or spits out of the window which is referred to, of course, as the "wind-oh" instead of the usual "winder".

'Here are a few pointers regarding T-customs at meals. It is un-T to bring your dinner wrapped in a newspaper or a coloured cloth. T-people always bring it in a brief-case but would consider a picnic basket as vulgarly ostentatious. In the same way flasks are vulgar, but bottles are T. It is un-T to arrive at dinner, as lots of people do nowadays, with a mug of whisky or beer in your hand which you have bought at a public house on the way, but the idea that T-people don't bring mugs to dinner, but rely on being provided with "glasses", is, of course, absurd except for very formal entertainments. In my father's time surnames were still used by T-people, especially among those who had not previously met, but the use of surnames would be considered to be disgusting un-T middle-class affectation at a dinner party today.

'Gramophones were still in use in Daddy's young days (he was born in 1984), and I asked him once if it was usual to have the gramophone on the table at dinner. Daddy thought seriously and told me that possibly in *his* father's time this had been the custom, but that in his own young days (before telepathic screens) the Television set was usually the chief object on the table apart from the sandwiches and tins and Coca-cola containers. On the cinema the dinner table is usually covered with "silver", which is the un-T description of "memorial cans". It must be fifty years since any T-people put one of those old horrors on the dinner table.

'It would be interesting to know the origin of so many false ideas about T-manners which people have, and which drive me literally mad with irritation. I think myself that it is because fiction writers and so on took no account of the change which seems to have come about when peers went into the Trades Unions in large numbers. At the time when this happened some people, incredible as it may sound today, rather resented this trend, on the grounds, according to Professor ffrench-Cable, that Trades Unions were working-class movements which ought therefore to have working-class membership. But the peers were wily birds, then as now; they knew that Trades Union membership was essential to their economic well-being, and I expect they dropped whatever manners and customs antagonized their critics most, and as usual the entertainment world never found out what the T-people were really up to. After the Amalgamation of the Country House Exhibitors Association with the National Treasure-Mongers Union in 1979 it was inevitable, given the high percentage of peers in the Labour Party, that peers should become the natural leaders of the T.U.C. At least that's what it says in Professor ffrench-Cable's book. Seven dukes have been T.U.C. Chairmen since 1979, thirty-eight Earls, fifty-six Viscounts, and, for some reason, only one marquess. Today there are only two dukes, four marquesses, fourteen Viscounts and two barons who do not belong to Trades Unions of any kind. Significantly these are the poorest peers, with an average income (according to Inland Revenue published figures) of about £250,000 a year, which is slightly lower than the minimum basic wage as established last year. One big T-point remains constant: nobody wants a really poor peer. It is very un-T not to be rich.'

HOW TO GET ON IN SOCIETY

by

JOHN BETJEMAN

HOW TO GET ON IN SOCIETY

Originally set as a competition in 'Time and Tide'

Phone for the fish-knives, Norman,
  As Cook is a little unnerved;
You kiddies have crumpled the serviettes
  And I must have things daintily served.

Are the requisites all in the toilet?
  The frills round the cutlets can wait
Till the girl has replenished the cruets
  And switched on the logs in the grate.

It's ever so close in the lounge, dear,
  But the vestibule's comfy for tea,
And Howard is out riding on horseback
  So do come and take some with me.

Now here is a fork for your pastries
  And do use the couch for your feet;
I know what I wanted to ask you —
  Is trifle sufficient for sweet?

Milk and then just as it comes, dear?
 I'm afraid the preserve's full of stones;
Beg pardon, I'm soiling the doilies
 With afternoon tea-cakes and scones.